Saving and
Investment
in a Global
Economy

Saving and Investment in a Global Economy

Barry P. Bosworth

The Brookings Institution
Washington, D.C.

Copyright © 1993
THE BROOKINGS INSTITUTION
1775 Massachusetts Avenue, N.W., Washington, D.C. 20036

Library of Congress Cataloging-in-Publication data

Bosworth, Barry
    Saving and investment in a global economy / Barry P. Bosworth
        p.   cm.
    Includes bibliographical references and index.
    ISBN 0-8157-1044-5 (alk. paper) : — ISBN 0-8157-1043-7
(pbk.)
    1. Saving and investment—United States.   2. Saving and
investment.   3. Competition, International.   4. United States—
Economic conditions—1981-   5. Economic history—1971-1990.
6. Economic history—1990-   7. Balance of payments—United States.
8. Foreign exchange rates—United States.   I. Title.
HC110.S3B67   1992
339.4'3'0973—dc20   92-35664
                                                        CIP

9 8 7 6 5 4 3 2 1

The paper used in this publication meets the minimum requirements of the American National Standard for Information Sciences—Permanence of Paper for Printed Library Materials, ANSI
Z39.48-1984

THE BROOKINGS INSTITUTION

The Brookings Institution is an independent organization devoted to nonpartisan research, education, and publication in economics, government, foreign policy, and the social sciences generally. Its principal purposes are to aid the development of sound public policies and to promote public understanding of issues of national importance.

The Institution was founded on December 8, 1927, to merge the activities of the Institute for Government Research, founded in 1916, the Institute of Economics, founded in 1922, and the Robert Brookings Graduate School of Economics and Government, founded in 1924.

The Board of Trustees is responsible for the general administration of the Institution, while the immediate direction of the policies, program, and staff is vested in the President, assisted by an advisory committee of the officers and staff. The by-laws of the Institution state: "It is the function of the Trustees to make possible the conduct of scientific research, and publication, under the most favorable conditions, and to safeguard the independence of the research staff in the pursuit of their studies and in the publication of the results of such studies. It is not a part of their function to determine, control, or influence the conduct of particular investigations or the conclusions reached."

The President bears final responsibility for the decision to publish a manuscript as a Brookings book. In reaching his judgment on the competence, accuracy, and objectivity of each study, the President is advised by the director of the appropriate research program and weighs the views of a panel of expert outside readers who report to him in confidence on the quality of the work. Publication of a work signifies that it is deemed a competent treatment worthy of public consideration but does not imply endorsement of conclusions or recommendations.

The Institution maintains its position of neutrality on issues of public policy in order to safeguard the intellectual freedom of the staff. Hence interpretations or conclusions in Brookings publications should be understood to be solely those of the authors and should not be attributed to the Institution, to its trustees, officers, or other staff members, or to the organizations that support its research.

Foreword

The emergence during the 1980s of large trade imbalances among the major industrial economies focused public attention on America's relationship to the economies of other countries. Exchange rates, current account balances, and other aspects of the international economy have become central to the design and conduct of economic policy.

The integration of the global economy through increased trade in goods and services has been under way for several decades. But the opening of national capital markets, with the consequent increase in movements of financial capital across borders, is more recent. The shift to a system of flexible exchange rates has made understanding the linkages between the domestic economy and the economies of other countries difficult.

In this study Barry Bosworth examines the causes of the trade imbalances of the 1980s. While much of the public discussion has emphasized microeconomic causes—specifically, what Americans perceive as the unfair trade practices of other countries—this analysis argues that the imbalances can be traced to macroeconomic changes in saving and investment in the major industrial economies.

Focusing on those economies, the author shows how changes in domestic saving and investment lead to changes in interest rates, exchange rates, and trade balances. He also examines the reasons for the decline in rates of national saving and investment throughout the industrialized world, and considers whether the recent wide fluctuations in exchange rates are a cause for concern or simply an integral part of the international adjustment to divergent patterns of national saving and investment.

Research for this book was financed in part by a grant from the Tokyo Club Foundation for Global Studies. Suzanne M. Smith provided extensive research assistance. The author is grateful to Rudiger Dornbusch,

Warwick J. McKibbin, George S. Tavlas, and several anonymous referees for helpful comments and suggestions. Hillary Sheldon assisted in the final preparation of the manuscript and verified its factual content. David Bearce also helped verify the manuscript. Irene Coray provided staff assistance. Deborah Styles edited the manuscript, and Florence Robinson prepared the index.

The views expressed here are those of the author and should not be ascribed to the officers, trustees, or other staff members of the Brookings Institution.

BRUCE K. MACLAURY
President

February 1993
Washington, D.C.

Contents

Tables

Figures

1

Introduction

Given the experience of the 1980s, we are all far more aware of the impact of foreign economic events on our economic welfare. Even countries as large as the United States can no longer afford to formulate economic policy without addressing its impact on economic relations with the rest of the world. National economies are now linked both through financial markets and the more traditional trade goods and services. Additional complexities have been introduced by the shift to a system of flexible exchange rates in the early 1970s and the gradual elimination of restrictions on international capital transactions.

Increased awareness has also been accompanied by greater controversy. This is particularly true with respect to the causes and consequences of the large trade imbalances among the major industrial economies that emerged during the 1980s. The United States, in particular, ran a cumulative current account deficit of nearly $1 trillion and in less than ten years went from the world's largest creditor to its greatest debtor. The emergence of this deficit, matched by equally large surpluses in Japan and Germany, represented a largely unexpected development in the global economy, which some economists predicted would spark a global crisis initiated by a collapse of the dollar. The United States, they said, would be forced to generate trade surpluses in the 1990s as foreigners, no longer willing to finance U.S. deficits, abandoned U.S. financial markets and demanded repayment of the debts run up during the previous decade. Although their crystal ball appears to have been a bit cloudy, the question remains whether such trading balances will be typical of the future and, further, what forces will be driving them.

Certainly the trade deficit has led to a growing disenchantment within the United States with the current arrangements governing international trade. Many American public officials attribute this deficit

1

to the unfair trade practices of other nations, blaming foreigners—particularly the Japanese—for the competitive problems of American industry. They have sought to correct the situation by restricting imports and pressuring other countries to purchase American exports. Others see the deficits as evidence of America's economic decline, of its inability to compete in global markets. They believe that U.S. industrial and trade policies should be redirected to promote the strategic position of American firms in the international economy. The United States, they argue, should abandon its multilateral approach to international economic issues and pursue a narrower concept of national advantage.

Public officials elsewhere have been more distressed by the great fluctuation in the exchange rates accompanying the trade imbalances. They complain that under the flexible exchange rate system the economic policies of deficit countries such as the United States have become undisciplined. They also fear that unanticipated variations in the exchange rate will discourage international trade and threaten the financial stability of the global system.

In contrast, most economists believe that trade practices are not the primary determinants of the imbalances. Rather, they put a large emphasis on the role of domestic patterns of aggregate saving and investment. The current account is defined as the difference between domestic saving and investment. Any economic entity—be it a household, a business firm, or a country—will have a net deficit in its external transactions when its expenditures exceed its income, or, equivalently, when it saves less than it invests. Thus countries such as Japan, whose saving exceeds their domestic investment needs, will have a surplus in their external transactions, whereas those such as the United States, whose low saving is less than their domestic investments, will have external deficits. Most economists, therefore, see the deficit as a reflection of macroeconomic factors and call for policies to increase the nation's rate of saving.

According to the orthodox economist, the root of the U.S. balance of payments problem lies in the sharp decline in the nation's rate of saving during the 1980s, which in turn can be attributed to a fall in private saving and a substantial increase in the federal government's budget deficit. The shortfall of national saving in relation to investment demands, combined with a monetary policy aimed at suppressing inflation, increased the competition for funds in financial markets and sent interest rates climbing. Foreign investors, attracted by the high returns, moved their funds into the United States. The increased foreign demand for dollars, required to invest in American markets, in turn drove up the value of the dollar and thus the price of American products in global markets. The result was a substitution of foreign for domestically produced goods—that is to say, exports declined and imports increased. As Americans began to spend more on imports than they earned from exports, the net supply of dollars to foreigners rose until it came into balance with the higher level of demand for dollars by foreign investors. Thus, the increased flow of foreign financial capital into the United States was matched by an equal deficit in the trade account. In that sense the United States financed a surge of consumption spending by borrowing from abroad or in later years by selling assets to foreigners.

This highly simplified outline of the links between the balance of domestic saving and investment and the current account camouflages a host of controversial issues about the direction of causality and the role of the exchange rate in the process. It also fails to reflect the extent to which the magnitude and sustainability of the external imbalances that developed during the 1980s surprised even the economists.

The purpose of this book is to examine the sources of the trade imbalances developed during the 1980s. A primary objective is to test the empirical validity of the three basic tenets of the conventional economist's view of the link between the domestic economy and a nation's external balance. The first question to raise in this regard is whether the development of current account imbalances is due to changed patterns of domestic saving and investment. In the United States it is common to refer to the twin deficits, that is, to tie the emergence of a current account deficit to the sharp increases in the government budget deficit and the consequent decline in national saving. Do similar arguments serve to explain changes in the current accounts of other countries?

Second, what are the primary factors governing the determination of exchange rates? Are changes in the exchange rate a response to differences in interest rates between countries? According to the standard model, domestic interest rates are an indicator of relative capital shortages, with high interest rates leading to an inflow of financial capital and an appreciation of the currency. Although there is considerable evidence to support this explanation for the appreciation of the American dollar in the early 1980s, its relevance to the general evolution of exchange rates remains unclear.

And third, to what extent do exchange rates influence trade flows?

The nominal exchange rate is a critical element in the definition of the relative price of domestic versus foreign-produced products. The failure to observe an immediate and large decline of the U.S. trade deficit following the fall of the dollar in the mid-1980s led to a revival of arguments that changes in the exchange rate were an ineffective—and according to some analysts, unnecessary—means of controlling the volume of exports and imports.

All three of these issues have been the subject of an enormous amount of empirical research, much of which has focused on the experience of the United States. This study, in contrast, examines the experience of a large number of industrial economies, treating each as a separate sample that can be used to test the generality of the basic assumptions of the standard model of international economic adjustment.

Changing Views of the Global Economy

A striking feature of the 1980s has been the fast pace at which the global economy has moved toward integrating what used to be a group of relatively independent economies free to follow their own economic policies in response to domestic concerns and problems. It is true that international trade in goods has been expanded throughout the post–World War II period, promoted by several multilateral agreements to reduce tariffs and other barriers to trade. The switch to a system of flexible exchange rates in the early 1970s and the gradual elimination of government restrictions on international capital flows in the 1970s and early 1980s represent more recent but equally important steps in that integration. Another significant change is that North America, although still one center of world trade and finance, no longer dominates the field. Japan in Asia and the Common Market in Europe have emerged as equally important centers of finance.

Before the 1980s current account surpluses and deficits were generally small and transitory. As several studies have pointed out, national saving and investment rates were closely linked, moving up and down together.[1] Many economists concluded that the international mobility of capital was limited, that each country was more or less an island, forced to live within its own means, dependent on its own saving to finance its own investment, and unable to borrow to any appreciable extent from other countries. The economic policy of the United States,

---

1. Feldstein and Horioka (1980).

in particular, was largely based on a closed economy model that paid little attention to international economic relations.

Thus, the Reagan administration's economic program of large tax cuts combined with increased defense spending initially seemed remarkably similar to the "guns and butter" program of Lyndon Johnson. To finance the budget deficit, the government had to borrow in capital markets. As a result, interest rates were expected to rise until the demand for domestic investment was pushed down to the level of the available saving, as government borrowing crowded business firms and potential home-buyers out of financial markets.[2] If the monetary authorities attempted to limit the rise in interest rates by expanding credit, the result would be inflation.

Those expectations could not have been more wrong—interest rates and inflation both declined throughout much of the 1980s. Something had obviously changed, most notably the relationship between the United States and the rest of the world. The break with past trends is reflected in the altered relationship between U.S. domestic rates of saving and investment over the period of 1965–90 (figure 1-1). Up to 1980 domestic rates of saving and investment did move up and down together, and the current account played a minor balancing role. During the 1980s there was a sharp break in this pattern. The net national saving rate fell sharply, from its historical average of 10 percent of net domestic product (NDP) to less than 3 percent by 1990. The initial decline was concentrated in the public sector, where the federal budget deficit ballooned to 5 percent of NDP, but in later years the decline was amplified by a fall in private saving. Meanwhile, domestic net investment climbed from its low of 3 percent of NDP in the 1982 recession to 7.8 percent in 1984, before beginning a gradual drift downward. The gap between domestic investment and domestic saving was filled by a large net inflow of resources from abroad that peaked at $154 billion, or 4 percent of NDP, in 1986.

The large American current account deficit has been an unexpected development that has greatly altered the traditional views of wealthy countries as creditors, supplying capital to poorer nations with greater unexploited investment opportunities. Most Americans still fail to grasp the fact that they are debtors, not creditors, in the global economy who depend on an inflow of foreign resources to support their living standards.

2. For a summary of the literature on fiscal crowding out, see Friedman (1978).

FIGURE 1-1. *U.S. Saving and Investment Rates, 1965–90*

Percent of net domestic product

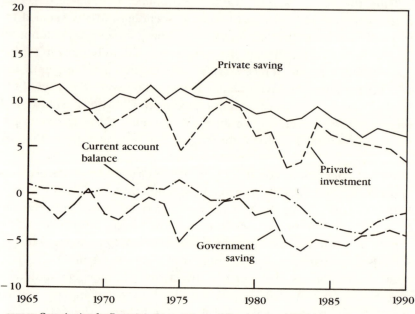

SOURCE: Organization for Economic Cooperation and Development (1991b).

International Capital Markets

What was not fully appreciated at the beginning of the 1980s was the extent to which the liberalization of controls on financial transactions would support the development of an international capital market. With the emergence of a global capital market, a nation's rate of investment is no longer constrained by its rate of saving: domestic investment can, if it offers a sufficiently attractive rate of return, draw on a pool of worldwide saving. By the same mechanism, a surplus of domestic saving can easily flow abroad if foreign markets offer a higher interest rate.

At the time few economists believed that the financing of the U.S. trade imbalance was technically feasible because international capital markets appeared severely limited in size. Even among the experts, there was a belief that the external imbalances posed a serious threat to the stability of the global economy. As already mentioned, some went so far as to forecast a collapse of the dollar, which was expected to bring on a global crisis.[3]

3. Marris (1985).

As the decade proceeded, however, these views changed considerably. Whereas at the beginning of the 1980s most economists were
emphasizing the limited potential for international capital movements,
ten years later many were asserting just the opposite, that, with the
removal of government controls on external financial transactions, capital had become fully mobile across national borders. The prevailing
view now is that capital markets are evolving from a set of loosely
linked national markets into a single global entity.

The developments in the international arena are analogous to the
growth of the national capital market among the states of the U.S. union.
Today, the United States does not even maintain records of financial
flows, regional differences in interest rates have virtually vanished, and
no one would argue that saving within an individual state has any
restraining effect on its rate of investment.

Although the world is still far from having a single capital market,
there is significant evidence of increased integration of national capital
markets. Many countries, beginning with the United States in the early
1970s, have reduced or completely removed restrictions on external
capital transactions. Note, too, the trend toward equalization of interest
rates across national capital markets and the growth in the volume of
international capital flows.

The equalization of interest rates across national borders is the most
commonly proposed measure of capital mobility. The international market, however, differs from a national capital market in one important
respect: the potential for variation in exchange rates. That is to say,
interest rates denominated in different currencies can never reach complete equalization because of the risk of capital gains and losses arising
out of changes in the exchange rates. It is possible, however, to compare
interest rates on financial instruments issued in different countries but
denominated in a common currency. Equalization of these interest rates
is referred to as closed interest parity. The effects of liberalization on
such rates are illustrated in figure 1-2. Geographical differences clearly
fade away here. For example, the differential between the interest rate
on Euro-dollar deposits and the domestic rate on three-month certifi-
cates of deposit has steadily narrowed since the early 1970s, when the
United States removed the last vestiges of controls on foreign capital
transactions.

In 1973–74 Germany removed restrictions on the inflow of capital
that had been designed to prevent nonresidents from acquiring German
assets. Under those restrictions, banks were prohibited from paying

FIGURE 1-2. *Offshore and Onshore Interest Rates, Selected Countries, 1970–91*[a]

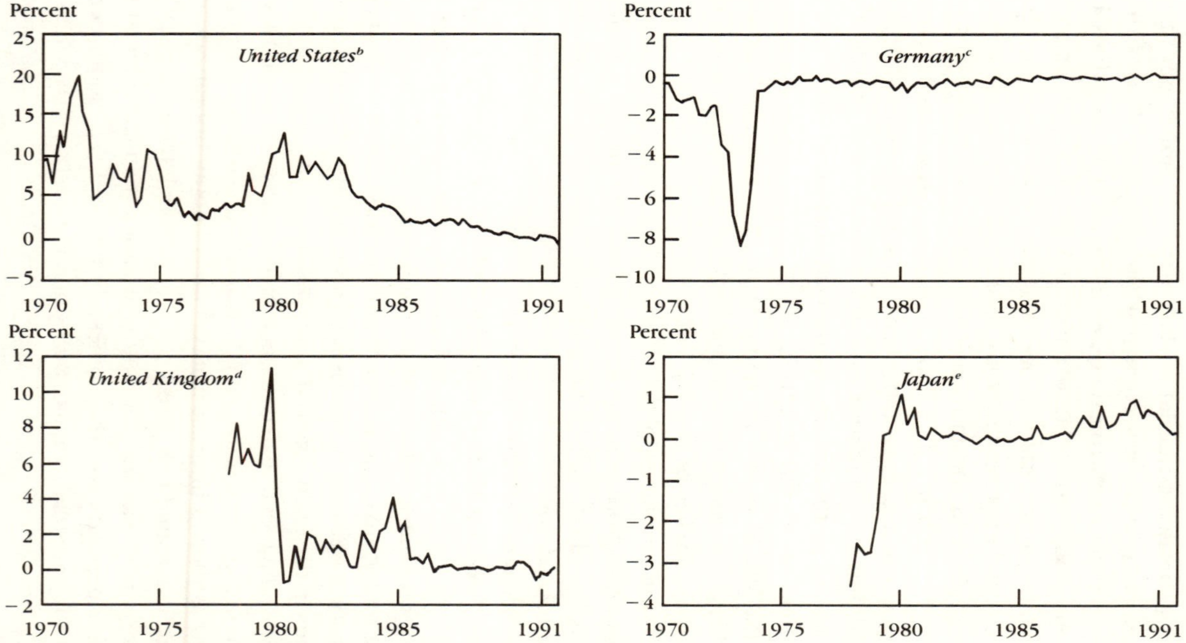

SOURCES: International Monetary Fund, *Financial Statistics* (Washington), data tape.
a. Interest rate differentials in percent per year.
b. Euromarket rate, three-month in U.S. dollars versus three-month CD rate.
c. Euromarket rate, three-month in deutsche marks versus three-month domestic money market rate.
d. Paris interbank offer rate on three-month deposits versus money market rate.
e. Euromarket rate, three-month in Japanese yen vesus three-month domestic money market rate.

interest to foreigners on large deposits, and nonresidents were not allowed to purchase German bonds.[4] Thus, when the German central bank adopted a stringent anti-inflation policy in the early 1970s, domestic interest rates exceeded comparable foreign market rates. After 1974 this difference virtually disappeared. Japan also suppressed financial investments by foreigners until 1979 because of a concern that the inflow of capital would lead to an appreciation of the yen and reduce international competitiveness. Again, the interest differential narrowed drastically after those restrictions were removed. A similar narrowing occurred when the United Kingdom took steps to liberalize controls on foreign accounts in 1979. In the 1980s other European countries, such as France and Italy, began to remove capital controls.

A comparison of interest rates denominated in a common currency is, of course, a very limited test of capital market integration because it fails to take into account exchange rate risk. Even so, the sharp narrowing of the interest differentials illustrates the importance of the prior restrictions on capital flows.

The growth in international capital markets can also be roughly estimated by examining the volume of cross-border financial transactions. Figure 1-3 compares the growth of international transactions in financial capital with that of trade in goods and services. For the countries of the Organization for Economic Cooperation and Development (OECD), international trade steadily increased, from 10 percent of total GDP in the mid-1960s to about 13 percent by 1990. Meanwhile, private capital transactions, measured as the average of gross inflows and outflows, grew rapidly, albeit from a very low base, from about 2 percent of GDP in the mid-1970s to more than 5 percent in 1990. Although not enough data are available to draw any firm conclusion about the outstanding stock of international financial assets and liabilities, international bank lending, which represented about 80 percent of the gross flow reported in figure 1-3, increased in relation to total gross domestic product (GDP) moving from 6 percent in the mid-1970s to 10 percent in 1980 and up to 17 percent by 1989.

However, international capital transactions should have expanded even further in the 1980s, if the many economists who have cited international capital mobility as cause of the large current account imbalances of the period are right. In fact, the gross flow of financial

---

4. The specific actions are discussed more fully in Frankel (1990) and the references cited therein.

FIGURE 1-3. *International Capital Investment and Trade for Industrial Countries, 1970–90*[a]

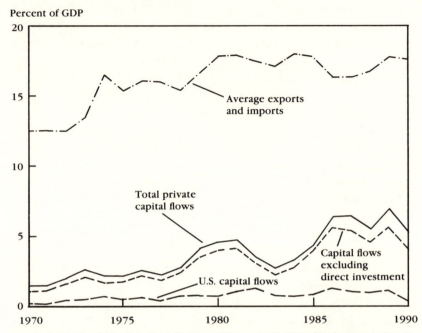

Percent of GDP

SOURCES: International Monetary Fund, *Balance of Payments Statistics* (Washington, various issues).

a. Trade flows are in current prices and 1985 exchange rates. Capital flows are in current prices and current exchange rates and are computed as an average of inflows and outflows.

capital declined in the early part of the decade, in large part because bank lending waned with the onset of the debt crisis in developing countries. Furthermore, if there is an international capital market, it is limited to the developed economies. They account for nearly all the growth in international capital transactions. In contrast, the developing countries have seen a reduction in their access to international capital; on net balance, they have been transferring resources to the developed economies. It is also important to note that the growth in direct investment by multinational firms has been relatively small.[5]

5. The data on annual changes in international financial assets and liabilities understate the growth in the volume of financial transactions of very short duration. Much of the activity reflects short-term speculation and hedging against exchange rate movements, rather than long-term lending. In addition, the data on direct investment are of limited value because firms often borrow in the financial markets of the countries in which they are operating.

The United States has played a surprisingly small role in the expansion of the global capital market. Indeed, the average of the gross flows of private financial capital in and out of the United States has expanded at a slower pace than it has for the industrial countries as a whole (figure 1-3). The U.S. trade deficit of the 1980s was financed by an increased inflow of foreign private capital, and the flow of U.S. investments abroad (indicated by a minus sign below) was largely unchanged as a share of GDP.

Element	1970s	1980s
U.S. Private Assets	− 1.8.	− 2.0.
U.S. Private Liabilities	0.9.	3.2.
Governments (Net)	0.8.	0.2.
Capital Accounts Balance	**− 0.1.**	**1.4.**
Statistical Discrepancy	0.1.	0.5.
Current Account Balance	**0.0.**	**− 1.9.**

Between the 1970s and the 1980s the average of the private gross flows into and out of the United States rose from 1.4 to 2.6 percent of GDP, and the net transactions of governments declined in importance.

Flexible Exchange Rates

The increased integration of capital markets is only one of the changes the international economy has experienced in recent years. Trade imbalances of the magnitude observed in the 1980s also presuppose an integration of goods markets. The process of borrowing abroad involves two distinct transfers: a transfer of financial claims to foreigners that operates through financial markets (the capital account), and a transfer of goods and services in the opposite direction (the current account). Both of these transfers are included in the balance of payments accounts, with the basic condition that any current account imbalance must be matched by an equal imbalance of the capital account. Even if financial capital may move freely across national borders, rigidities in the process of freeing up goods in the lending country and moving them to the borrowing country can create problems of completing the transfer when the proceeds of the loan are spent.

The fact that a loan is financed by funds from abroad has no effect on the spending plans of the borrower. The proceeds of the loan will be spent on a mix of domestic and foreign-produced goods in the same fashion as a loan obtained from domestic sources. Part of the transfer of goods will occur automatically as the level of demand in the recipient country increases, part of which will fall on imports. Most of the marginal dollar of expenditures, however, is spent on domestic goods. Thus, the remainder of the transfer will need to be accomplished by inducing a switch in the composition of overall expenditures from domestic to foreign goods. This change in the composition of demand requires an increase in the relative price of domestic versus foreign-produced products in the recipient country. If buyers view foreign and domestic goods as close substitutes and are very willing to switch between the two sources of supply, the magnitude of required price change will be small.

In reality buyers do not appear to view domestic and foreign goods as close substitutes, and changes in aggregate trade flows require rather large changes in relative prices. The U.S. trade deficit of the mid-1980s, for example, which reached a peak of 4 percent of GDP, was associated with a roughly 30 percent rise in the relative price of American-produced goods in world markets.

Under the pre-1971 system of fixed nominal exchange rates, changes in relative prices could occur through a rise in the overall level of domestic prices in the borrowing country. The domestic political consequences of that price inflation often served to discipline governments, forcing them to adjust their fiscal and monetary policies so as to bring domestic demand into line with domestic supply, thereby eliminating the need for a trade deficit. It is possible that within a fixed exchange rate regime, the large U.S. trade deficit of the 1980s would not have occurred. Public anger over the domestic inflation would have forced the government to reverse the highly stimulative fiscal policy that it adopted in 1981.

In a world of flexible exchange rates, however, the price of domestic goods in relation to foreign goods can be shifted through a simple change in the nominal exchange rate. The short-run consequence of such a move may be considered desirable by consumers, for an appreciating currency implies cheaper imports, low inflation, and a higher standard of living. The costs show up as lost jobs when workers in the tradable goods industries lose out to workers in other countries; but many will undoubtedly blame their problems on the unfair competition of foreigners. Clearly, introduction of a system of flexible exchange rates was as significant as the existence of an international capital market for financial capital because it created the potential for the large changes in relative prices needed to shift trade in goods and services without the disruptions typical of sharp variations in the domestic price level.

In summary, the distinctive features of today's international economy are (1) close links between national economies, both through trade in goods and services and flows of financial capital, and (2) a flexible exchange rate regime. The trade in goods and services is an old story, but the growth of international financial markets is a more recent development. In some respects the degree of integration of financial markets now exceeds that of goods markets: financial capital flows among some economies appear to be more sensitive to variations in relative interest rates than the flow of trade to changes in relative prices. The system of flexible exchange rates was designed to provide national economic authorities with greater autonomy over their own economic policy, but it also increased the extent of the integration by facilitating the change in relative prices required to reallocate goods and services internationally.

Sources of Controversy

The interpretation of current account imbalances as being driven by changes in domestic patterns of saving and investment is not free of controversy even among economists. To begin with, the statement that the current account is the difference between saving and investment simply reflects an accounting identity. It implies nothing about causation. It gives no indication, for example, of whether a nation's current account deficit might have arisen because other nations have surpluses, forcing a realignment of domestic saving and investment. On a global basis, current account balances must sum to zero. Thus, an autonomous inflow of capital from surplus countries could lead to low domestic interest rates and thereby encourage domestic investment and consumption. The result would be a shortfall of domestic saving in relation to investment, a currency appreciation, and a current account deficit; but the driving force would be the changes in external economic conditions.

If the current account is to be interpreted as largely a reflection of domestic economic conditions, domestic rates of saving and investment should evolve in a predictable fashion that is not directly influenced by foreign events. If either of these components of the identity is highly irregular, the framework would have limited analytical value. Thus, it is important to examine the behavior of domestic saving and investment and to determine the sources of change. That analysis can help us determine whether the imbalances that emerged in the 1980s are a transitory phenomenon or indicative of patterns that can be expected to continue into the future.

Second, the mechanism by which a shift in the domestic saving-investment balance translates into an alteration of the current account remains in dispute. According to the conventional view an excess of domestic investment in relation to saving should prompt a rise in the interest rate. A higher domestic rate would in turn induce an inflow of capital from abroad and a bidding up of the exchange rate. An appreciation of the exchange rate in turn implies a rise in the cost of domestically produced products in global markets. The higher relative cost of domestic products would then lead to a substitution of foreign for domestically produced goods. The key assumptions in this story are that the exchange rate responds in a regular and predictable fashion to variations in the differential between domestic and foreign interest rates, and that trade flows are strongly affected by changes in real exchange rates. If interest rates have little effect on exchange rates, or if changes in the real exchange rate have little effect on trade flows, the conventional model and its policy prescriptions lose their credibility.

In this conventional view, changes in the exchange rate are a necessary part of the process by which the current account is brought into line with a changed saving-investment balance: the real exchange rate needs to change to induce a substitution of foreign for domestically produced products. As a carryover from the era of fixed exchange rates, however, changes in nominal exchange rates continue to smack of illegitimacy, in part because some observers believe that the flexible exchange rate system weakens the constraints on governments to avoid inflation. They argue that currency devaluation is too easy a means of avoiding the consequences of excessive inflation. A few economists go even further and argue that exchange rate adjustments are an unnecessary part of the adjustment mechanism: in their view, a current account imbalance can be eliminated solely through a realignment of domestic saving and investment, without significantly changing the relative price of domestic and foreign-produced products.[6]

The conventional interpretation has also come under attack because of what critics have judged to be a disappointingly small response of trade flows to the decline of the dollar between 1985 and 1987. The

6. McKinnon (1984) and Mundell (1991).

United States began the decade with a rough balance in the current account. By the mid-1980s the deficit had soared to $150 billion, in a supposed response to the sharp rise in the exchange rate. Yet, even when the real exchange rate returned late in the decade to the level of 1980, the deficit remained close to $100 billion. Obviously, there is still considerable doubt about how well the model actually performs at the empirical level in accounting for the evolution of current account balances over the 1980s.

Although previous studies have dealt with these issues, they have focused primarily on the experience of the United States. Yet in many respects the United States plays an unusual role in the world economy, both because of its size and the extent to which it occupied center stage throughout the post-World War II period. That position is now being challenged by other countries that are catching up to it economically; indeed, several other nations have emerged as economic centers of nearly equal importance in what has become a more diverse global economy. Thus the experience of the United States alone cannot be used to judge the degree of global economic integration or the adequacy of any given interpretation of macroeconomic events.

In an effort to remedy the situation, this study evaluates the empirical support for several key concepts of the conventional model by using data from fifteen diverse industrial countries. With a larger empirical base of analysis, we can hope for a more insightful assessment of the extent to which the basic model provides a consistent explanation of global economic developments. By testing the various hypotheses against the experience of a large number of countries, we reduce the probability of obtaining spurious correlations and conclusions.

The discussion opens in chapter 2 with some basic concepts concerning the accounting framework of the balance of payments and a summary of the Mundell-Fleming model that forms the basis of the conventional view of open-economy macroeconomics. This model was developed in the early 1960s and extended in several dimensions over the next few decades. It is designed to analyze the consequences of alternative fiscal-monetary policies in a world in which nations trade with one another and are linked together through international capital markets. The model is essentially an extension of the IS-LM concept of a closed economy that supported much of the policy analysis of earlier years, and it is often used in the formulation of macroeconomic policies.

The following chapters evaluate three critical aspects of the conventional model of international economic adjustment: the behavior of domestic rates of saving and investment, the determinants of exchange rates, and the influence of exchange rates on trade flows.

The Domestic Saving-Investment Balance

Chapter 3 highlights recent changes in the patterns of domestic saving and investment in the industrial countries. Although the decline of the saving rate within the United States has attracted widespread attention, a similar falloff has been occurring in other countries. Outside the United States, however, the investment rates have declined even more than the rates of private saving, leaving most industrial countries with a surplus of private saving over private investment rather than a shortfall. The principal purpose of chapter 3 is to examine the international consistency of a variety of explanations that have been put forth to explain the decline in the rates of saving and investment.

As the chapter explains, the variations in current account balances have actually been rather small, given the wide fluctuations in rates of private saving, private investment, and government budget balances. Variations in the three domestic components appear to have been linked in some offsetting fashion resulting in relatively small changes in the net balance. Either they are influenced by a common set of determinants, or the claims of highly integrated global markets are premature and there are still substantial barriers to the free flow of resources across national borders.

One common factor is the overall rate of economic growth, which is found to have a strong positive influence on rates of both private saving and investment. Such a result is expected for investment because of strong theoretical considerations linking growth in the capital stock to the rate of growth of output. More surprising is the notion of a positive association between saving and long-run rates of income growth, because most current explanations of saving behavior assume that saving is negatively related to the expected rate of income growth.

A sustained change in output growth has a much stronger impact on investment than on private saving, so that there is a persistent tendency for the excess of saving over investment in the private sector to be negatively related to the rate of economic growth. This is reflected in the emergence of a large private-sector saving surplus in most industrial countries following the pronounced slowing of economic growth after the 1973 oil crisis. If that had been all that was going on, these countries would have had large current account surpluses after 1973.

The excess private saving did not spill over into the external sector, however. It was absorbed instead by a large increase in government budget deficits. For most of the countries in the sample, there is a strong negative correlation between budget balances and the private saving-investment balance, even after cyclical influences on the budget are excluded. This raises the possibility that governments target the current account in setting their policies, or that barriers to large current account imbalances force them to adopt compensatory policies to sustain domestic employment. An effort is made to resolve this issue in chapter 3 by relating policy-induced changes in the budget balance to the current account and domestic unemployment, but with little success.

The United States is one country for which the above argument makes little sense because there was no tendency for private saving to exceed private investment after 1973. Nor can the large government budget deficit of the 1980s be traced to a surplus in the private saving-investment balance.

Several other potential determinants of saving and investment behavior were tested for the significance of their statistical correlation with the observed data, and the results are reported in chapter 3. Except for a strong correlation between variations in interest rates and investment, these tests were largely negative. Factors that did not emerge with a consistent correlation with rates of private saving included inflation, demographic changes, and capital gains on existing assets.

In summary, there are some regularities in the behavior of private saving and investment that should have strong implications for the current account balance. In particular episodes of high output growth should be reflected in current account deficits, and surpluses should emerge during periods of low growth. Such a pattern does not emerge on a regular basis, however, because of offsetting actions of governments to alter the public-sector saving balance. It remains unclear whether the actions of governments are a predictable response to slow growth and rising unemployment in the domestic economy, or a reflection of a desire to maintain a current account balance near zero.

The Determinants of Exchange Rates

The effort in chapter 4 to account for observed changes in exchange rates yielded mixed results. On one hand, an important element of conventional theories of exchange rate behavior was confirmed in that differences in the rate of price inflation have a marked effect on the trend in a country's nominal exchange rate. Price-level differentials had consistently significant coefficients in equations explaining the nominal exchange rate, and in many cases the coefficients did not deviate significantly from the value of unity that would be expected from the purchasing power parity condition.

On the other hand, it proved more difficult to verify the effect of interest rate differentials on the exchange rate. This relationship is critical to the argument that the real exchange rate of countries with a shortage of saving in relation to investment will appreciate in order to attract resources from abroad. For about half of the countries in the sample, there was a strong positive correlation between the exchange rate and the differential between domestic interest rates and a trade-weighted average of rates in other countries. For several other countries, however, the correlation had limited statistical significance. More serious problems were found for the United Kingdom and Japan. In the case of the United Kingdom, the exchange rate and the interest rate differential consistently displayed an unexpected negative correlation with high statistical significance. In the case of Japan, there was a strong negative correlation between the exchange rate and foreign interest rates, but no evidence of a positive correlation with any domestic interest rate.

The United States stood out as providing the strongest support for the orthodox explanation of changes in exchange rates. It was possible to account for a large proportion of the variation in the dollar's value over the 1970s and 1980s, although the sharp currency appreciation of late 1984 and early 1985 is not fully explained.

In forecasting future exchange rates the estimated models perform only marginally better than a simple hypothesis relating the current real exchange rate to its own prior value for intervals up to a year; but they do provide a better explanation of the evolution of the exchange rate over longer periods of time. Thus, empirical results confirm, in part, the conventional model, but a significant amount of variation remains unexplained.

Trade Flows

The strongest support for the conventional model of the links between the domestic and global economy is provided by the analysis of trade flows in chapter 5. There is substantial evidence that changes in real exchange rates produce strong and predictable effects on the trade balances of all of the industrial countries.

Even so, the results differ somewhat from those of earlier studies in that variations in income growth turned out to have a smaller effect on trade flows and the effect of differences in relative prices is greater. The smaller role for income changes is attributable to the use of industrial production rather than GDP to measure the demand for imports. The use of GDP, which includes many nontraded goods, systematically understates the short-run variation in the demand for tradables, requiring the assignment of a larger income elasticity. In contrast, the larger price elasticities appear to result from the effort to control for measurement errors in previously used price indexes, which introduced a downward bias to estimates of the price elasticities.

The results of the empirical analysis are also somewhat surprising when viewed from the perspective of current discussions of trade policy. The effect on trade flows of changes in real exchange rates are large for both the United States and Japan, and the adjustment of trade flows has also been very substantial in both. I found no evidence that the post-1985 adjustments have been smaller than the historical data would lead one to expect. Contrary to popular perceptions that Japanese exports and imports are determined by non-market forces, the overall price elasticity is somewhat larger for Japan, and the changes in its trade balance in response to global economic forces have been greater than that of the United States.

Policy Implications

The results of the analysis summarized above have implications for several current policy issues. First, a recurring theme in discussions of the global economy is the need to coordinate the fiscal-monetary policies of the major industrial countries. The reasoning in support of such coordination is heavily based on the model of the linkages between domestic saving and investment, exchange rates, and trade flows that underlies this study. In 1985 the G-7 countries initiated a set of coordinated macroeconomic policies aimed at reducing the trade imbalances that had built up in prior years, Thus, the experience after 1985 represents an interesting test both of policy coordination and the standard interpretation of the sources of trade imbalances.

Second, the results of this study can be used to examine some of the issues surrounding the concern about the emergence of a global capital shortage in future years. Real interest rates were abnormally high throughout the 1980s; and, with expected high capital costs of economic reconstruction in Eastern Europe and the former Soviet Union, there are concerns that capital could become increasingly scarce in the 1990s, further raising global interest rates.

Policy Coordination and Post-1985
Current Account Adjustment

The expansion of economic links among countries has made it more difficult for policymakers to manage their own economies, as the effects of one country's actions spill over to other countries through changes in exchange rates, trade, and capital flows. For example, the integration of global financial markets, combined with a system of flexible exchange rates, implies that fiscal policy is an increasingly ineffectual tool of short-run stabilization policy. Unless it is believed to be purely temporary, the financing of a budget deficit raises interest rates and the exchange rate, leading to an offsetting decline in the trade balance as well as domestic investment. While the evidence of this study indicates that we have not reached a stage of complete financial market integration, the reactions to the fiscal policies of the United States in the early 1980s suggest that a very large proportion of any fiscal stimulus will be dissipated into the global economy within a short period of time. Between 1982 and 1985 the U.S. budget deficit, exclusive of cyclical factors, increased by $127 billion as part of a program to stimulate the domestic economy. With a lag of about one year, however, that stimulus was largely offset by a $110 billion increase in the trade deficit.

Macroeconomic policy coordination is a potential means of improving outcomes by expanding the range of policy options. Governments can trade off changes in their own policy for changes by others. They can incorporate the spill-over effects into their evaluation of policy options and reduce the risk that individual nations will attempt to pass the costs of adjustment off onto others.

Excessive emphasis on policy coordination, however, can have undesirable effects. It may lead nations to delay policy adjustments that are in their own self-interest in the pursuit of coordinated actions in which others will bear a larger portion of the costs. Governments may also attempt to avoid responsibility for poor domestic economic policies by blaming foreigners for their own failings. Furthermore, the successful coordination of macroeconomic policies requires a degree of consensus about economic goals and how the global economy operates that has yet to emerge.

These issues are illustrated by the effort to coordinate the macroeconomic policies of the major industrial countries over the last half of the 1980s. The growing fear in economic circles of an impending financial crisis led the finance ministers of the G-5 countries to meet at the New York Plaza in September 1985 to adopt a coordinated policy for reducing their current account imbalances. The experience after 1985 also serves as an interesting test of the conventional view of the adjustment process. Did adjustment occur? The answer on the whole appears to be yes, but for reasons that had less to do with the actions of the governments involved than is commonly supposed.

First, the surge in the dollar exchange rate came to an end well before the Plaza accord. In retrospect, the sharp runup of the dollar in late 1984 has the characteristics of a speculative bubble in the exchange market, which is by and large unexplained by any change in the underlying fundamentals. Although, as shown in chapter 4, a standard exchange rate model can account for nearly all of the dollar's rise between 1981 and 1984 and for the fall over the last half of the 1980s, the spike in early 1985 is unexplained. The episode also lasted for so brief a period that it had little effect on trade flows. It follows that much of the initial decline was also equally unimportant for trade.

The United States, the largest deficit country in the sample, promised to correct its budget imbalance as a way of increasing its national saving. And, at first, it made some progress in this direction. As shown in table 1-1, the U.S. budget deficit declined from 5.3 percent of NDP in 1986 to a low of 3.7 percent in 1989 before going back up. The reduced budget deficit, however, was largely offset by a decline in private saving. The national saving rate was actually lower in 1989–90 than in 1985. While the current account deficit did shrink substantially after 1987, it occurred primarily as a consequence of a decline in the private investment rate. By the mid-1980s the U.S. economy had absorbed the huge fiscal stimulus of 1981-82, and a slowing of overall growth and high real interest rates began to exert a toll on investment.

Despite American criticism that Japan was not doing enough to reduce global trade imbalances, the Japanese current account surplus shows a much larger adjustment, declining from 5.2 to 1.7 percent of NDP between 1986 and 1990. Again, the source of the adjustment is the change in private sector balances. The Japanese government sharply increased its overall budget surplus from − 0.1 percent of NDP to 4.1 percent. If the Japanese government did anything, it settled on an easy monetary policy that held down interest rates in the face of a huge

TABLE 1-1. *Saving-Investment Balances of the Leading Industrial Economies, 1985–90*

Percent of net national product

Year	Government budget	Private saving	Domestic investment	Current account	Non-Oil trade
United States					
1985	− 5.0	8.3	6.5	− 3.3	− 2.4
1986	− 5.3	7.5	5.9	− 3.7	− 3.0
1987	− 4.3	6.2	5.6	− 4.0	− 3.0
1988	− 4.1	7.3	5.3	− 2.8	− 2.0
1989	− 3.7	6.8	4.9	− 2.2	− 1.1
1990	− 4.2	6.4	3.5	− 1.8	− 0.5
Japan					
1985	0.2	12.6	8.5	4.4	9.0
1986	− 0.1	13.1	7.9	5.2	7.0
1987	1.6	11.8	8.6	4.4	5.8
1988	2.9	12.0	11.0	3.4	4.3
1989	4.1	11.0	12.1	2.5	3.5
1990	4.1	11.4	13.5	1.7	3.2
Germany					
1985	0.4	8.7	6.2	3.0	9.3
1986	0.0	11.2	6.2	5.1	8.4
1987	− 0.7	11.7	6.3	4.7	7.7
1988	− 1.1	13.4	7.5	4.8	7.4
1989	1.6	12.6	8.9	5.4	7.6
1990	− 1.2	14.6	9.8	3.6	7.6
Europe					
1985	− 3.7	10.8	6.5	0.6	4.9
1986	− 3.7	11.1	6.5	1.0	3.6
1987	− 3.2	10.3	6.9	0.3	2.7
1988	− 2.6	10.7	8.3	− 0.3	1.9
1989	− 2.0	10.4	8.9	− 0.5	2.0
1990	− 2.7	11.3	8.6	− 0.2	2.3

SOURCES: Organization for Economic Cooperation and Development (1991b) and author's calculations as explained in the text. Construction of the data is explained more fully in chaps. 3 and 5.

boom in private domestic investment, but this action was probably motivated as much by a belief that low interest rates would limit the appreciation of the yen as by a desire to accelerate domestic demand growth.

Within Germany, the other large surplus country, little happened to change economic policy between the conclusion of the Plaza agreement and the fall of the Berlin Wall. The government did act to adopt a slightly more stimulative fiscal policy in 1987–88, but it was largely absorbed by an unexpected rise in the private saving rate, and it was reversed in 1989. The German current account surplus rose sharply in 1986 and remained at a high plateau throughout the remainder of the decade. Instead, adjustment occurred in the rest of Europe: many countries began to run significant deficits in their trade with Germany, primarily as a counterpart of the recovery in rates of private investment. For Europe as a whole, the current account surplus declined by about 1 percent of NDP, but it was the result of a pickup of private investment demand, and governments continued to emphasize fiscal restraint.

At the same time, the G-5 governments did promote strong overall expansion of GDP up until 1990. Furthermore, the reduction of U.S. interest rates relative to those of other countries allowed its exchange rate to decline. From a saving-investment perspective, however, the basic story is one of surging private investment in the surplus economies and declining investment in the deficit economy, the United States—not exactly what the finance ministers had in mind.

The adjustment process worked best in precisely the area that was subject to the greatest criticism. There was a very large realignment of trade flows in response to the change in real exchange rates. In part, that realignment received little attention because of the impatience of policymakers and various commentators: the largest portion of the change did not emerge until some time after exchange rates were realigned. The analysis of trade flows in chapter 5, however, provides no evidence that the trade adjustments were systematically smaller after 1985 than one might have expected from trade behavior up to 1985. While the lags in the response of trade to relative price changes were long after 1985, they do not appear to have been greater than in the past. Note, too, that the sharp fall in oil prices in 1986 camouflaged some of the changes that were occurring in the portion of the trade balance most affected by real exchange rates. As shown in the last column of table 1-1, the non-oil trade deficit of the United States declined by 2.5 percent of NDP between 1986 and 1990, whereas the Japanese surplus fell by 5.8 percent of NDP, and that of Europe by 2.5 percent. The relative magnitudes of the adjustment also seem surprising in view of the widely espoused argument that the Japanese economy is closed to outsiders and that its trade is unresponsive to exchange rate changes.

The large trade imbalances among the industrial countries and wide fluctuations in exchange rates during the 1980s did impose substantial costs on the global economy. However, criticism of the international economic system as the cause of those problems seems misplaced. The fundamental sources of the imbalances were within the domestic sectors of the United States. The international adjustment process itself worked surprisingly well.

A Global Saving Shortage?

The debate over current account imbalances in recent years has pushed the international policy debate in the direction of the belief that all current account imbalances are bad. Current account surpluses and deficits are seen as equally unacceptable and the apparent standard for policy is to aim for balance.

The emergence of such a policy rule seems strange, however, given the simultaneous growth of an international capital market. The existence of a capital market eliminates the need for each economic entity to aim for balance in its own transactions. An international capital market should lessen the concern of nations about the current account balances of others; and, combined with flexible exchange rates, reduce the need for explicit policy coordination.

Rather than focusing on a simultaneous reduction of current account surpluses and deficits in the mid-1980s, an alternative policy would have simply called on the United States to act in its own interest to raise its national saving and reduce its borrowing from the international market. The result would have been a decline in global interest rates, and a reallocation of capital flows from the United States to other potential borrowers, such as the developing countries. Given the high level of global interest rates, it is not clear why the simpler policy was not the better policy.

At the time, several arguments were made in favor of the standard of current account balance. Some economists contended that a cutback of demand growth in the United States would lead to a slowing of global economic growth rather than a reallocation of saving. Others perceived the international capital market as being limited to facilitating the flow of funds among the industrialized economies with only a small capacity for financing the needs of developing countries. The industrializing economies of Asia were not faced with capital constraints, as their own internal saving is more than adequate to finance growth; and the chaotic condition of many Latin American countries made them unattractive to international capital markets as candidates for current account deficits.

Furthermore, the extent of international integration of capital markets can be exaggerated. The analysis in this study suggests that global capital markets are increasingly linked, but they are far from being fully integrated. The concept of a single market into which all saving flows and from which investments, regardless of location, can be financed is not a reality.

There is also a concern that current account imbalances place excessive political pressures on the international trading system. Trade imbalances become entangled with the issue of jobs: exports are good because they create jobs, and imports are bad because they destroy jobs. For example, American politicians perceive the trade deficit not as a reflection of the inadequacy of U.S. saving but as a result of unfair trade measures of others. The result has been pressure on high saving countries such as Japan either to reduce their saving or to absorb the saving within the domestic economy.

On the other hand, the sustained high level of real interest rates since the early 1980s provides strong evidence that the basic problem facing the global economy is not a surplus of saving. Instead, the disappearance of the large current account surpluses of the OPEC countries, the emergence of new capital needs associated with economic reconstruction in the formerly socialist countries, and the reemergence of substantial investment opportunities in Latin American countries all suggest the possibility of a future global shortage of capital. In the short run abrupt increases in aggregate saving raise the risk of recession because of lags in the process of shifting the resources freed up by higher rates of saving into increased investment. These short-run concerns, however, should not obscure the fact that rates of return on capital have been rising, not falling, in the 1980s and early 1990s.

How should we think about the issue of a future global saving shortage? First, it is difficult to provide a definitive measure of global capital needs. In general, rates of saving and investment have fallen significantly in the industrial countries over the last two decades. As discussed in chapter 3, however, much of the decline appears to be a natural result of slower rates of aggregate income growth. Slower rates of income growth imply a reduced need for additional capital and lower rates of both saving and investment. The lower rates of growth in income can be traced, in turn, to smaller rates of increase in the labor force of the industrial countries and a reduced rate of technical change. Thus we should not interpret lower rates of either saving or investment as indicative of a capital shortage.

A more reasonable point of reference would be to look at interest rates, adjusted for inflation, as a measure of the relative availability of capital. From this perspective there was evidence of a shortfall of capital availability during the 1980s. An estimate of the average long-term real interest rate for the G-5 countries was computed by deducting a five-year centered average of the rate of change of GDP price deflators and using relative GDPs in 1980 to obtain the weighted average. The resulting measure of global interest rates averaged 2.5 percent in the 1960s, declined to less than 1 percent over the last half of the 1970s, and rose to over 5 percent in the 1980s. Even in the recession years of 1991–92 the estimated real rate was only slightly below 5 percent.

The increase in real interest rates also occurred at a time when most developing countries had been forced out of international capital markets, both by the high costs of borrowing and their own internal economic problems. For example, the net current account deficit of the Latin American countries, one measure of the net inflow of capital to the region, averaged only 1 percent of GDP in 1983–90, compared with 3.6 percent in the 1975–81 period. More significantly, these economies were unable to attract new capital sufficient to meet the interest payments on their old debt. As a result, they actually transferred a significant portion of their resources to the richer industrial economies, with an average annual trade surplus equal to 2.7 percent of GDP in the 1983–90 period. Nearly all of this resource transfer was at the cost of sharply lower rates of investment within Latin America. The annual rate of growth of investment spending fell from 7.4 percent in the 1970s to − 3.1 percent in the 1980s.[7]

Looking ahead, the need to finance economic reconstruction of in the former socialist economies, together with a resolution of the debt crisis that restricted international lending to the developing economies in the 1980s, suggests the possibility of added pressures on interest rates in the 1990s. However, it is easy to generate excessively large estimates of the potential for such international lending. Few nations are able to achieve net capital inflows on a sustained basis equal to more than 2–4 percent of their GDP. On this basis, optimistic estimates of the net capital inflow of Eastern Europe and the former Soviet Union would be $50 billion to $75 billion annually in the mid-1990s; and net lending to Latin America equal to 3 percent of GDP would add approximately $30 billion. Thus the potential magnitude of added external capital needs of these regions seems small when measured against the $3.4 trillion of total investment within the OECD in 1990. Instead,

7. Inter-American Development Bank (1992), p. 288.

pressures on capital markets will be determined largely by developments within the industrial countries. Uncertainties in the projections of the U.S. government budget deficit, for example, are greater than those associated with any estimates of net lending to the former socialist economies.

The current account surplus of Germany and the deficit of the United States largely disappeared during the early 1990s, leaving Japan as the only large economy with a major current account imbalance. Internal costs of unification will probably prevent the return of significant German surpluses in the near term. The outlook for the United States is more problematic, however. The current account deficit was reduced by a sharp curtailment of domestic investment, not by an increase in domestic saving. Economic recovery in future years is likely to raise investment and push the United States back toward a larger current account deficit. Within Japan, the boom of private investment spending, which led to a decline in its current account deficit in the late 1980s, proved to be unsustainable. However, the shift toward larger public sector saving surpluses, adding to national saving, is unlikely to continue in the 1990s. Japan is being pressured by its trading partners to consume more domestically. These uncertainties about developments within the industrial economies suggest the lack of any firm basis on which to make clear forecasts of future capital market conditions. Much depends on the government economic policies within the major industrial countries. If, for example, the United States continues to be unable to resolve its public budget deficit, its borrowing would sustain a high level of real interest rates in the future.

Conclusion

The basic theme of this study is that the conventional model of international macroeconomics works surprisingly well in explaining economic developments over the 1980s. A perspective that emphasizes divergences between domestic rates of investment and saving as the primary driving forces behind changes in the current account can account for a large portion of the imbalances that developed during the 1980s. Furthermore, an adjustment process that links domestic changes in saving and investment to changes in interest rates, exchange rates, and ultimately trade flows is evident in the historical data for the industrial countries that were examined in this study. Despite criticism of the international trade system, the results of this study strongly support the view that exchange rate changes are an effective and necessary means of realigning trade balances.

At the same time, much remains unexplained, particularly in the area of exchange rate determination. The determination of domestic rates of saving and investment is also more complex than commonly believed, with the behavior of governments being particularly hard to explain. Exchange rates are also subject to substantial variation that is not well explained by existing hypotheses.

One major conclusion is that current account imbalances, such as those that emerged during the 1980s, should not be treated as an abnormality nor as evidence of an impending disaster. They will become an increasingly common feature of the international economy. With the greater international mobility of goods and financial capital, there is little reason—from either a normative or a positive perspective—to expect future rates of national saving and investment to be closely linked. The task for international economic policy is to develop institutions and policies capable of managing those imbalances and ensuring that they do not become a source of global instability. The task for national economic policy is to understand the ways in which global economic integration changes the rules of the game and the perspective from which alternative policy options need to be evaluated. This latter task may be particularly difficult for the United States to carry out, given its rather insular approach to economic policy up to now.

Another point to emphasize is that the current account balance should not be a direct target of government policy. Changes in the current account should be perceived as symptoms of underlying changes in the domestic economy. As the global economy continues on the path of integration, the current account will become a simple reflection of imbalances between domestic saving and investment. If no effort is made to identify the reasons for the changed domestic balance, it will be impossible to determine whether any given current account balance is good or bad. For example, suppose that a current account deficit arises from a boom of domestic investment opportunities that exceeds the supply of domestic saving. The ability to obtain additional saving from a global market is clearly a positive development in such a situation. Even if a current account deficit were a reflection of a decline in domestic saving, it would still make no sense to scale back domestic investment to force a realignment with the lower rate of saving. Nations should care about their rates of saving and investment, not the current account.

Finally, it is evident that the international economic system is still in a stage of major transition. While the international linkages between national financial markets have expanded, they are not yet fully integrated. There is not a global capital market in the same sense that we speak of a single national market within the United States. Goods markets also are not fully integrated in the sense that substantial changes in real exchange rates, greater than could be achieved solely through variations in domestic inflation rates, are still required to achieve the realignments of trade balances that are likely to be common in the future. This suggests that a flexible exchange rate system will continue to be a critical feature of the system for some time to come.

The trend toward a more open global economic system will also have profound effects on the conduct of macroeconomic policy. The combination of more integrated capital markets and a flexible exchange rate system will reduce the effectiveness of fiscal policy as a tool of stabilization policy. Instead, the perspective on fiscal policy will have to shift toward a greater concern with the balance of national saving and investment over the longer term. On the other hand, monetary policy will become a more effective regulator of total demand through the potential to influence exchange rates and thus trade flows.

2

An Analytical Framework

Integration of the global economy has long been a goal of American foreign policy, but Americans have been slow to recognize the implications of the changes, particularly as they affect their own economic policies. Economies are now linked through financial markets as well as trade in goods and services. Economic policies that worked to stabilize jobs and incomes in a relatively closed economy can have dramatically different effects in an open global trading system in which we must worry about their effects on exchange rates and other determinants of our competitive position. Fortunately, the effort to understand the operation of this type of economic system and its implications for policy does not have to start from scratch. There is an extensive body of theoretical and empirical research on the subject, undertaken over the past several decades by specialists in international macroeconomics.

As mentioned earlier, the purpose of this chapter is to introduce some basic concepts and to outline the framework of the Mundell-Fleming model, which specifies the ways in which international markets alter the behavior of national economies. Thus the model can be used to identify the critical issues involved in explaining the origins of current account imbalances and the consequences of changes in fiscal and monetary policies. Some readers, already familiar with those issues, may prefer to skip this chapter.

Alternative Measures of the Current Account

Much of the controversy over the causes of current account imbalances and their implications for economic policy has arisen because there are alternative ways of describing the current account itself. If it is defined as the difference between receipts (exports) and payments (imports) to foreigners, for example, attention is drawn to factors that have a direct effect on trade flows, such as trade policies, relative prices, and domestic and foreign income growth.

The current account can also be defined as the difference between a nation's saving and its domestic investment, which leads to a completely different set of concerns about the causes of changes in domestic saving and investment. This definition underlies the so-called twin-deficits view, according to which the swelling U.S. budget deficit of the 1980s and its reduction of national saving were the primary cause of the current account deficit.[1]

Still a third definition sees the current account as the change in a country's net foreign assets. Within the overall balance of payments any surplus or deficit on the current account must be matched by an equivalent and offsetting financial flow on the capital side of the accounts. Therefore, disturbances to the current account balance could be viewed as the product of changes within capital markets. A definition that emphasizes the capital side of the balance of payments focuses on factors such as differences in the levels of national interest rates, financial deregulation, and capital flight—all of which lead investors to alter the allocation of their investments between domestic and foreign assets.

All three of these concepts are equally relevant measures of the current account. Each accentuates a different aspect of an economic system in which interacting events in both the domestic and global economy determine the current account.

External Balance

To begin with, the current account (CA) summarizes all transactions with foreigners arising out of current production activity. It includes three main kinds of external transactions: net trade in goods and services $(X - IM)$, net factor income receipts (NFI), and net transfer payments (NTR):

$$(2\text{-}1) \qquad CA = (X - IM) + NFI + NTR.$$

Most discussions of external economic relations focus on trade in goods and services, and the latter two components are less well understood.

---

1. Feldstein (1984).

Net factor income consists largely of capital income earned on the stock of overseas investments minus the payments made on foreign investments in the domestic economy. The net foreign investment position of a country equals the cumulation of past current account surpluses plus any capital gains or losses. In the period 1945–80, for example, the United States had consistent surpluses on its current account and by the end of 1980 had accumulated net foreign assets valued at about $380 billion. Then during the 1980s it borrowed $1 trillion in the form of current account deficits, and its net foreign asset position fell to − $480 billion at the end of 1990.[2] The result has been a sharp decline in net factor income.[3] Transfer payments consist largely of foreign aid and items such as foreign payments to the United States to finance the Gulf War.

Trade in goods and services constitutes the largest and most volatile component of the current account. Consequently, the current account balance would appear to be greatly influenced by changes in the determinants of exports and imports: foreign income (Y_f), domestic income (Y_a), and the relative price of foreign versus domestically produced goods (q),

$$(2\text{-}2) \qquad\qquad NX = f(Y_a, Y_f, q).$$

The concept of the real exchange rate provides a simple measure of relative prices, and it is defined as the nominal exchange rates (e) multiplied by the ratio of the foreign and domestic price levels (P_f/P_a):[4]

$$(2\text{-}3) \qquad\qquad q = e \cdot (P_f/P_a).$$

2. In 1990 U.S. assets abroad with direct investment valued at replacement cost totaled $1.764 trillion, and foreign investment in the United States totaled $2.176 trillion. See Scholl (1991).

3. Net factor income payments of the United States are not as negative as might be expected from its status as a debtor country because American firms earn a high rate of return on their overseas direct investments, whereas foreign investors have generally done badly in the United States. In addition, net factor income is often understated in balance of payments statistics because countries obtain more accurate information about interest paid to foreigners than the interest income received by their residents. For further details, see International Monetary Fund (1987).

4. In practice some ambiguity arises in choosing a specific price index to compute the real exchange rate. The problem is that broad measures such as the GDP deflator or the consumer price index include the prices of many goods and services that are not traded internationally. Yet narrow concepts, such as a price index for exports, may not reflect competitive conditions if firms simply price to the international market and absorb any cost disadvantage in reduced profits. This issue is addressed more fully in later chapters. In this chapter I follow the standard convention that defines the nominal exchange rate as the domestic currency price of a unit of foreign currency. Thus, a rise in e or q implies a domestic currency devaluation.

Internal Balance

The second measure of the current account highlights the relationship between a nation's current account balance and its domestic saving and investment. This definition follows directly from the basic identity of the national accounts, namely, that total domestic output (GDP) is equal to the sum of consumption expenditures (C), government spending (G), investment (I), and exports (X) minus imports (IM),

$$(2\text{-}4) \qquad GDP = C + G + I + (X - IM).$$

If we assume that all government spending is for consumption, the identity can be rewritten as

$$(2\text{-}5) \qquad (X - IM) = (GDP - C - G) - I, \text{ or}$$
$$= S - I;$$

That is to say, the trade balance is equal to domestic saving minus domestic investment.

In actual practice the situation is somewhat more complex because the residents of a country earn income from overseas activity, as well as from domestic production. Thus national accounts distinguish between gross domestic product (GDP) and gross national product (GNP), where the latter includes the net factor income earned by residents from overseas activities. In addition, net transfers are added to both sides of the identity. The result is a small redefinition of national saving, S:

$$(2\text{-}6) \qquad CA = (GNP - C - G + NTR) - I, \text{ or}$$
$$CA = S - I.$$

Thus, any current account (external) imbalance is precisely matched by an imbalance (internal) between domestic saving and investment.

Table 2-1 illustrates the structure of this identity for two contrasting countries, the United States and Japan. By international standards, the United States has had a relatively low private saving rate matched by a correspondingly low rate of private investment. Japan has high rates of both saving and investment. Before 1980, however, the balance for both countries resulted in small current account surpluses. The U.S. domestic saving rate fell from an average of 9 percent in 1976–79 to 3.3 percent in 1984–89, and the country incurred a large current account deficit to finance a rate of domestic investment that was itself below

TABLE 2-1. *Saving-Investment Balance, United States and Japan, Selected Periods, 1960–90*
Percent of net domestic product

Item	1960–73	1976–79	1984–90
United States			
National saving	10.6	9.0	3.3
Private saving	10.2	10.1	7.4
Government saving	0.4	− 1.1	− 4.1
Domestic investment	9.9	9.2	6.0
Private investment	8.4	8.8	5.6
Government investment	1.5	0.4	0.4
Current account	0.6	− 0.1	− 2.9
Statistical discrepancy	− 0.1	0.1	− 0.2
Japan			
National saving	26.1	18.2	18.9
Private saving	19.2	15.8	12.0
Government saving	6.9	2.4	6.9
Domestic investment	25.7	17.6	15.2
Private investment	20.9	11.2	9.9
Government investment	4.8	6.4	5.3
Current account	0.6	0.9	3.5
Statistical discrepancy	0.2	0.3	− 0.2

SOURCES: Organization for Economic Cooperation and Development (1991b) and author's calculations as explained in the text. The data for net investment by government in Japan are not fully compatible with other countries because of incomplete depreciation accounts. In addition, military expenditures are classified fully as consumption in the standard national accounts.

that of previous decades. Japan's domestic saving rate actually increased slightly in the 1980s—mainly because of a sharp rise in government saving—while the domestic investment rate continued to decline from the very high levels of the 1960s. Only in the 1980s did a large surplus emerge as a consistent characteristic of Japan's current account.

Another closely related concept concerning the relationship between the current account and the domestic economy defines total domestic demand or absorption (A) as the sum of consumption, government spending, and investment. Hence, in this view, the current account is also equal to the difference between total income and domestic spending,

$$(2\text{-}7) \qquad CA = GNP - A + NTR.$$

Countries will have a current account deficit when they spend (absorb) more than they earn.

The concepts embedded in equations 2-6 and 2-7 are equivalent since both are derived from the expenditure identity of the national accounts. They differ only in that equation 2-7 focuses on the difference between income and total spending, whereas equation 2-6 emphasizes the difference between investment and consumption.

The Capital Account

The above measures of the current account take into account only some of the economic links among national economies. In particular, they ignore the issue of how a surplus or deficit is to be financed. A current account surplus implies that a nation is accumulating claims on foreigners, and a deficit can be financed only by selling off assets or by borrowing from foreigners. Thus, from the financial side (capital account) of the balance of payments, the external balance can also be measured as the change in the nation's net foreign assets (B), that is to say, its assets minus its liabilities,

$$(2\text{-}8) \qquad\qquad CA = B_t - B_{t-1}.$$

Throughout much of the post-World War II period governments restricted private foreign exchange transactions primarily to those required to finance trade or direct investment, and they covered variations in the current account by altering their own foreign exchange reserves. Beginning in the 1960s the regulation of private capital flows was gradually liberalized. Today, most industrialized countries and some developing economies allow full convertibility for all transactions in foreign exchange. The result has been a rapid growth of private cross-border financial investment, and these capital account transactions have contributed at least as much as current account transactions to the variations in the demand and supply of foreign exchange.

In practice the reported current account will not precisely equal the change in the value of a country's net foreign assets. The valuations of asset holdings are subject to capital gains and losses that are not included in the current account. Furthermore, it is more difficult to obtain accurate data on financial transactions than on trade in goods and services. As a result, there can be a large statistical discrepancy between measures of the current account based on goods transactions and the corresponding measure based on reported financial transactions.

As already pointed out, the balance of payments identity requires that the net flow of foreign exchange from current account transactions be matched by an equal net flow on the capital account, which is defined to include both private capital transactions and the official settlements of governments. These two net flows represent distinct sets of economic behavior, determined by different underlying relationships. Although most discussion of changes in the current account is concerned with the determinants of exports and imports, the capital account emphasizes the importance of financial market conditions. Excluding official reserves, the capital account reflects the decisions of private agents as to the allocation of their wealth between domestic and foreign assets. Thus emphasis must also be placed on factors that affect those investment decisions, such as relative interest rates and expected exchange rate changes. Much of the complexity surrounding the links between national economies and their implications for policy results from the fact that the current and capital accounts are determined by different factors but in the end must be equal.

Another point to make clear is that none of these accounting identities themselves imply anything about causation. Although the current account is equal to the difference between domestic saving and investment, this relationship does not rule out, for example, the possibility that changes within foreign economies, operating through the current account, can cause changes in the balance of domestic saving and investment.[5] Difficulties in the export sector can affect both saving and investment through reduced levels of aggregate income and production, and domestic interest rates are not independent of foreign rates.

In reality the trade balance, saving, and investment are all interrelated parts of a system in which the relative importance of domestic and foreign factors can only be evaluated through an empirical model that accounts for the changes in saving, investment, and trade flows. Several empirical models have been developed in recent years, but economists still cannot fully agree on the appropriate model structure and thus the policy implications that emerge.[6]

Nearly all of these models begin from a common theoretical point of departure, the Mundell-Fleming model of open economies that trade

5. Such arguments are advanced by several analysts who attribute the U.S. deficit to policy changes in Germany and Japan. See Aliber (1991). Similarly, economists in Germany and Japan argue that their current account surpluses were caused by the U.S. deficit rather than their own internal policies. See, for example, Ueda (1987).

6. See, for example, the evaluation of several multicountry models provided in Bryant and others (1988) and McKibbin and Sachs (1991).

with one another and are linked through international financial markets. Although the following description simplifies the basic model, it captures the important distinction for macroeconomic policy, namely, between a closed economy and an economy that is linked to a larger global economy.

The Mundell-Fleming Model

The Mundell-Fleming model is a direct extension of the IS-LM analysis popularized by J. R. Hicks to examine the determination of aggregate demand in a closed economy. The two major additions are the introduction of the real exchange rate as a determinant of net exports and the use of the accounting requirement for balance of payments equilibrium as the framework for summarizing the forces that determine the exchange rate.[7] The model is most simply illustrated under the assumption of constant prices with the following three equations:

(2-9)
$$Y = E(\overset{+\ -}{Y,r}) + NX(\overset{+\ -\ +}{q,Y,Y^*})$$

(2-10)
$$M = P \cdot L(\overset{+\ -}{Y,r})$$

(2-11)
$$NX - \dot{B}(\overset{-\ -\ +\ -\ +}{B,r,r^*,q,\dot{q}}) = 0.$$

In the notation all foreign values are denoted with an asterisk and are assumed to be exogenous. The sign of the partial derivative is denoted above each symbol.

Equation 2-9 summarizes the conditions for equilibrium in goods markets where total production (Y) is equal to domestic expenditures (E) plus net exports (NX). Domestic expenditures are positively related to income and negatively to the interest rate (r). The determinants of net exports are represented by domestic income, foreign income, and the real exchange rate (q). Net exports are negatively related to domestic income (increased imports) and positively related to foreign income (increased exports). A rise in the real exchange rate, that is, a depreciation of the domestic currency, is assumed to increase net exports.

---

7. Mundell (1963) and Fleming (1962). Useful expositions of the model with more recent extensions are provided by Tobin and Macedo (1980), Frenkel and Mussa (1985), and Marston (1985).

The domestic demand for money balances is set equal to an exogenously determined supply in equation 2-10, and is related positively to income (Y) and the price level (P) and negatively to the interest rate (r). At this point the model differs only slightly—through the addition of a relationship to determine net exports, from the traditional IS-LM model that dominated so much of post-World War II macroeconomic thinking.

The added complexity results largely from the need to specify the conditions for balance of payments equilibrium between the net inflow of funds from current account transactions (NX) and the change in the net stock of claims on foreigners, $\dot{B}$ in equation 2-11.[8] A current account surplus must be matched by a willingness of domestic investors to hold the additional claims on foreigners. That will depend primarily on the return on foreign bonds (r^*) in relation to the domestic rate (r) plus any expected gain or loss from expected changes in the exchange rate. The capital gain element is represented by the difference between the current exchange rate (q) and the expected future rate ($\bar{q}$). An increase in the domestic interest rate relative to the foreign rate will reduce investors' willingness to hold foreign assets. Thus, if the current and capital accounts are to remain in balance, a rise in income, which will reduce the current account surplus through increased imports, should be associated with a higher domestic interest rate and thereby reducing the demand for foreign assets.

This simple version of the model ignores the supply side of the economy and important lags and other aspects of the process. In particular, it focuses on flows and ignores the relationship between interest rate differentials and the allocation of the *stock* of wealth between domestic and foreign assets. It also fails to include a mechanism for determining the expected future, or equilibrium, exchange rate ($\bar{q}$).[9] This version should be thought of as applying over a period of a few years—long enough to allow for lags in the adjustment of trade to exchange rate, but not so long that the effects of stock accumulation become large. Finally, it pertains only to small economies because it overlooks any feedback effects from the domestic economy to the global economy and back to the domestic economy.

8. In the interest of simplicity the formulation of the current account ignores factor income payments and transfers and is equal to the trade balance.

9. A more complete exposition of the model with important extensions is provided by Frenkel and Razin (1987).

FIGURE 2-1. *Mundell-Fleming Model, Fixed Exchange Rate*

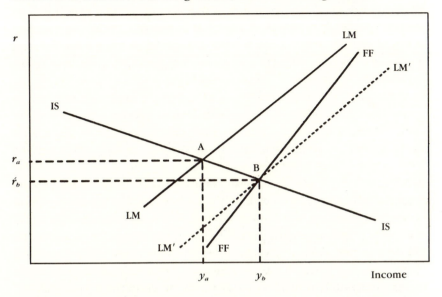

A Graphical Interpretation

The model is illustrated graphically in figure 2-1. The IS curve represents the combinations of the interest rate and income consistent with equilibrium in the domestic goods market (equation 2-9), and it is drawn on the assumption of a given exchange rate. It slopes downward and to the right because a lower interest rate is associated with higher levels of domestic spending and output. A rise in the exchange rate, making foreign goods more expensive, causes the curve to shift out to the right.

The LM curve is the combination of r and Y consistent with equilibrium in the money market (equation 2-10). It is upward sloping since a higher interest rate frees up money balances, which can only be reabsorbed by increasing the level of output and thus the transactions demand for money.

The FF curve displays those combinations of r and Y for which the trade balance is just matched by the net accumulation of foreign bonds (equation 2-11). It is this relationship that indicates the key role played by international capital markets. To the left of the curve, lower income, the trade balance generates a net inflow of foreign exchange in excess of the amount that investors are willing to hold. The converse condition holds to the right. If private capital transactions are not permitted, the FF curve would be a vertical line at the level of income where import demand precisely matched the level of exports, a zero trade balance. It could deviate from a zero trade balance only to the extent that governments were willing to accumulate foreign currencies. In any case it would be unaffected by the interest rate.

At the opposite extreme, financial capital is highly mobile across national borders. If investors regard foreign and domestic bonds as very close substitutes for one another in their portfolios and they have static exchange rate expectations, the FF curve will be a horizontal line at a level of the domestic interest rate equal to the foreign rate. Any trade deficit, associated with a rise in income, could be financed by a trivial increase in the interest rate since the higher rate would attract a flood of foreign financing. In the more intermediate case, shown in figure 2-1, there is a positive relationship between income and the interest rate because an increase in income moves the trade balance toward deficit (higher imports), and a higher domestic interest rate is required to induce investors to switch from foreign to domestic bonds to finance the imports.

Equilibrium is determined in the short run by the intersection of the IS and LM curves at point A. This is the standard result of the closed-economy analysis. At this level of output, however, the current account generates a surplus that exceeds the increment to foreign assets that investors are willing to absorb—A is to the left of the FF curve. If the monetary authorities wish to maintain a fixed exchange rate, they would need to continuously purchase the excess foreign exchange. The growth of domestic money required to finance those purchases would gradually shift the LM curve to the right until it intersected with the IS and the FF curve at B. Thus, under a fixed exchange rate regime, surplus countries would be required to follow a policy of monetary expansion, by lowering interest rates and raising income.

Alternatively, under a flexible exchange rate regime in which the monetary authorities do not intervene, the excess supply of claims on foreigners will cause the price of foreign exchange to fall, an appreciation of the domestic currency. The decline in the relative price of foreign goods would reduce exports and raise imports, causing both the IS and the FF curves to shift to the left, until equilibrium was established at lower levels of the domestic interest rate and output along an unchanged LM curve.[10]

10. This illustration has been constructed on the assumption that the initial equilibrium, A, occurs at a level of income to the left of the FF curve. If the initial intersection

Yet a third possibility is that the monetary authorities might intervene in the exchange market to buy foreign exchange but might finance their purchases by the sale of domestic bonds rather than increasing the money supply. In this case, which is known as sterilized intervention, the government could continue to remove the excess flow of foreign exchange from the market, and thus prevent any appreciation of the exchange rate, despite substantial current account surpluses.[11] This option does not exist for deficit countries because they would ultimately run out of foreign exchange.

The model can also be used to illustrate the implications of growth in international capital markets and greater capital mobility. When investors view domestic and foreign bonds as close substitutes, the FF curve becomes increasingly horizontal at the level of the world interest rate, r^*. A domestic equilibrium at an interest rate above the global rate is not sustainable because it would result in a huge capital inflow. The adjustment under a fixed exchange rate rule, outlined in figure 2-1, is not a gradual one because the central bank is overwhelmed and the LM curve jumps out until it passes through the IS curve at its intersection with the global interest rate. Under a flexible exchange rate regime, the inflow of foreign capital would cause a sharp currency appreciation, a deterioration of the net trade position, and a leftward shift of the IS curve until it intersects with the LM curve at the level of the world interest rate.

An allowance for domestic price flexibility would complicate the analysis, but not fundamentally alter the conclusions. In the fixed exchange rate example, the rise in domestic demand occasioned by the monetary expansion would lead to higher domestic prices, a real exchange rate appreciation, and an induced reduction in the current account surplus. As a result, the IS and the FF curves would shift to the left, output would decline, and the domestic interest rate would gradually recover to the world level as the current account surplus declined. In the flexible exchange rate example, the initial currency appreciation

---

of the IS and LM curve were to the right of the FF curve, where the current account surplus is less than investors' demand for foreign assets, the whole process would work in reverse, because there market pressures would induce a devaluation, a rise in q.

11. Taiwan is an example of a country that followed such a policy for many years. The government directed deposits of domestic savings into U.S. securities as a means of holding down the real exchange rate and promoting exports. Taiwan had large trade surpluses in the 1980s, and by 1987 it had a portfolio of roughly $50 billion in American financial assets, which exceeded 75 percent of its GDP. The policy was effective in promoting a rapid growth of exports, but the cost was huge capital losses when the dollar depreciated.

and fall in demand for domestically produced products would lower prices, and thereby increase the money supply in real terms, shift the LM curve to the right, and gradually raise output. Thus, the introduction of domestic price flexibility tends to reduce the distinction between fixed and flexible exchange rate regimes, blending the two together.

Implications for Saving and Investment

The effects of open international capital markets are most clearly seen in the implications of a shift in domestic demand. From the perspective of the Mundell-Fleming model, increases in government expenditures, private consumption, and investment are all equivalent, and they are represented by a shift of the IS curve to the right, as in part A of figure 2-2. The initial effect would be a higher level of domestic output at the intersection of the new IS curve with the unchanged LM curve at point B. The net output gain here is positive, but it is limited by an induced increase in the domestic interest rate, the movement along the LM curve. The extent of the offset coming from higher interest rates depends on the interest elasticity of the demand for money. The higher level of income will raise saving in both the public and private sector, and the higher interest rate will depress spending until domestic saving and investment are brought back into balance. That is the standard result under the traditional closed-economy analysis.

In an open economy, however, the external repercussions must also be taken into account. The increased income will lead to a deterioration of the current account through an increase in imports. Although the higher domestic interest rate will also induce a compensatory inflow of foreign capital, the two flows need not match a priori. Four potential outcomes can be distinguished, depending on whether the monetary authorities attempt to maintain the exchange rate or allow it to freely change and within each of those situations whether international capital movements are restricted or very responsive to differences in rates of return among markets.

FLEXIBLE EXCHANGE RATES. If capital mobility is so limited that the FF curve is more steeply sloped than the LM curve, as in part A of figure 2-2, the initial inflow of capital will fall short of the deterioration in the trade account, and the exchange rate will depreciate. The depreciation will in turn cause exports to increase and imports to decline, and this will magnify the impact on domestic output of the initial demand

FIGURE 2-2. *Effect of a Demand Stimulus, Flexible Exchange Rate*

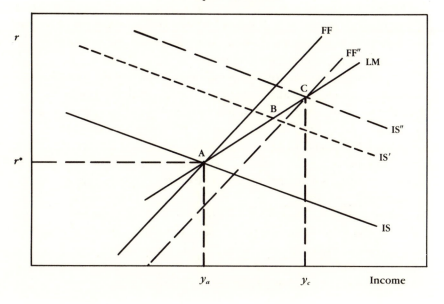

A. Low capital substitution

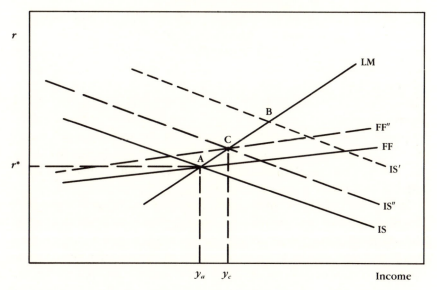

B. High capital substitution

stimulus (shifting the IS curve further to the right). In addition, the exchange rate decline and improvement in the trade balance will cause the FF curve to shift to the right, until a new equilibrium is established at an even higher level of domestic output and a higher interest rate. The outcome is represented in part A of figure 2-2 by the intersection of IS″ and FF″ at point C along an unchanged LM curve.

In contrast, if international capital movements are very sensitive to differences in interest rates—that is, if the FF curve is more horizontal than the LM curve—the capital inflow will more than cover the deterioration of the current account, and the exchange rate will appreciate, as indicated in part B of figure 2. This will reverse the direction of the secondary shifts in the IS and FF curves. A high degree of international capital mobility will dampen, rather than magnify, the changes in domestic output and interest rates. In effect, a larger portion of any change in domestic demand will spill over into the global economy through induced changes in the exchange rate, with less effect on domestic output. In the extreme case of perfect substitution between domestic and foreign bonds, represented by a horizontal FF curve, variations in domestic demand will have no effect on domestic output.

PEGGED EXCHANGE RATES.   If the central bank is committed to a specific exchange rate, it is forced to take steps to ensure that any increase in demand for foreign exchange for the purchase of imports is matched by capital inflow. If capital mobility is low—that is, if the FF curve is steeply sloped—the authorities will need to respond to the deterioration of the trade balance by restricting the domestic money supply and further raising interest rates. That would be equivalent to shifting the LM curve back until it intersects with the new IS curve along an unchanging FF relationship. If the capital inflow is high, that is, if the FF curve is relatively flat, the authorities will need to respond in the opposite direction: relieving the pressures on the exchange rate by purchasing foreign exchange and supplying additional reserves. Thus, the LM curve will shift outward, reversing a portion of the initial interest rate increase.

In summary, a high degree of international capital mobility greatly alters the economy's response to shifts in domestic demand, but the direction of change depends on the exchange rate regime. Under a fixed exchange rate system, monetary policy must be devoted to maintaining external balance, to equating the demand and supply of foreign exchange at the current exchange rate. Changes in domestic demand actually have a greater impact on domestic output and prices because the monetary authorities are forced to follow an accommodative policy to prevent any induced changes in the domestic interest rate. In contrast, under a flexible exchange rate regime monetary policy need not respond, and most real shocks to the domestic sector, identified by shifts in the IS curve, will quickly spill over into the global economy, rather than be absorbed domestically. A positive shock will continue to be reflected in some upward pressure on domestic income and the interest rate, but in addition the real exchange rate will appreciate, and the current account balance will deteriorate further. Declines in domestic saving, for example, will not force a compensatory reduction in domestic investment but will be offset by a net inflow of financial and other resources from abroad, and the result will be a current account deficit.[12]

Major Issues

The Mundell-Fleming model is widely used as a basic analytical framework for illustrating the role of macroeconomic policies in a global system of interrelated economies. Because it is only a framework for analysis, however, the policy conclusions that it suggests depend on the values assigned to the various parameters. As a result, although economists agree on how to approach the issues, they still disagree on fundamental causes of the current account imbalances that emerged during the 1980s, the reasons for their sustainability, and the possible effects of alternative policy measures.

One of the problems is that many are still divided over old issues pertaining to closed economies. They differ, for example, over the extent to which flexible wages and prices can ensure that an economy will operate near full employment, the stability of the money demand relationship, and the importance of expectations and the process by which they are formed. With the shift in attention to separate national economies linked together through international markets in goods and

---

12. A high degree of international capital mobility also greatly changes the roles of fiscal and monetary policy. Under a fixed exchange rate regime, monetary policy must be devoted exclusively to maintaining external balance, and it plays no role in domestic stabilization; fiscal policy actually becomes more effective in changing domestic output because monetary policy must respond to prevent an induced change in domestic interest rates. Under flexible exchange rates, however, it is fiscal policy that ceases to affect domestic output and employment as the demand changes are dispersed into the global economy.

financial capital, economists have had to deal with a host of additional complications.

They are in greatest disagreement over two key parameters of the model: the extent to which domestic and foreign goods substitute for one another, trading in a single market at a uniform price; and the extent to which domestic and foreign bonds substitute for one another in investors' portfolios, trading in a global capital market where interest rates on equivalent assets are equalized. The first issue is at the heart of the debate over purchasing power parity. The second arises out of a more abstruse concern with the condition of uncovered interest rate parity. These issues reflect differing views on the extent to which national economies have become integrated into a single global system.

Purchasing Power Parity

"Purchasing power parity" (PPP) is a term used to indicate that domestic and foreign goods are perfect substitutes. It represents an extension of the "law of one price" to a market basket of all goods. In an integrated competitive market, identical goods should trade at the same price when measured in a common currency. If private agents were very willing to switch between domestic and foreign goods in response to small changes in the relative prices of each, competition would ensure that these prices were equal when expressed in a common currency. International auction markets for primary commodities provide an example of close adherence to the law of one price.

When applied to exchange rates, PPP leads to the conclusion that a country's nominal exchange rate must be equal to the ratio of the domestic (P) and foreign price levels (P^*), or

$$(2\text{-}12) \qquad\qquad e = P/P^*.$$

Abstracting from transfer costs, the equilibrium real exchange rate is a constant.

PPP is important to consider because if domestic and foreign goods are close substitutes, demand could be reallocated between domestic and foreign production even with extremely small changes in real exchange rates. In such a situation flexible exchange rates would not be an important part of the international adjustment mechanism. A small change in the domestic price level in response to an innovation in domestic demand would be sufficient to disperse the impact of the demand change into the global economy.

At the same time, there are several obvious reasons why PPP might not apply in its most extreme form. First, most industrial products are highly differentiated, as producers try to set their products off from the crowd. By doing so, producers can establish higher price-cost margins in those market segments where competition is weak. Thus, few products are truly identical in different countries.

If price-cost margins are stable over time, however, the relative prices of two market baskets of differentiated products should not vary greatly over time if they are subjected to similar cost changes.[13] The potential for price substitution between differentiated products that fulfill a similar function is still high. Thus, it is more common to state PPP as a relative concept in which changes in the exchange rate are proportionate to changes in relative price levels.

Second, price indices include many products and services that are not subject to international arbitrage.[14] However, if the producers of tradable and nontradable goods purchase labor and raw materials at identical prices domestically, changes in the prices of their goods should differ only to the extent that they differ in their rates of growth of total factor productivity. Thus, if PPP holds at the level of tradable goods, a measure of PPP based on economy-wide prices might still apply if an allowance was made for a secular drift due to differing rates of technological change between tradables and nontradables.

Third, the composition of goods that enter into the construction of an aggregate price index will vary significantly across countries, for they neither consume nor produce the identical mix of products. Since the prices of all products need not change by identical amounts, indexes of the aggregate price levels may diverge because they are weighted differently. This could be a serious problem during periods of major change in relative prices, but is less important in adjusting for episodes of general inflation that are largely induced by monetary disturbances.

Actual experience during the 1980s with large changes in real exchange rates provides strong evidence that the basic assumption of PPP that domestic and foreign goods are close substitutes does not hold in the short or intermediate term. The reasons for the limited degree of substitution are less evident, however. In part, it has to do with the

---

13. Changes in the real exchange rate may lead to significant changes in competition or the price elasticity of demand faced by individual firms because an exchange rate appreciation permits a larger number of foreign firms to enter the market.

14. Lawrence (1979) and Marston (1986) provide illustrations of the extent of departure between the overall price level and the price of tradables in Japan.

behavior of firms in the traded goods sector. These firms—doubting that the change in the exchange rate will persist and facing significant fixed costs in altering the scale of their production—simply vary their price-cost margins in order to stabilize the level of their demand. Thus, they raise their margins when their home currency depreciates and reduce prices to meet the competition when the currency appreciates.[15] The result is limited movement in the volume of trade. As for buyers, their response to small changes in relative prices is often to display a strong attachment to traditional sources of supply or a preference for domestic producers and not to shift the pattern of their purchases. Specific markets that do display a high degree of substitution between domestic and foreign sources of supply often become candidates for government intervention in the form of quotas because of the concentrated nature of the impact on domestic employment.

The usefulness of PPP as a long-term assumption remains an open issue. Most of the explanations for a low degree of substitution in the short run would seem not to apply or to become far less important over a longer period of time. Yet, empirical studies of trade flows do not suggest that lags alone account for the relatively low degree of price substitution.

The debate over adjustment policies hinges on the extent of price substitution between domestic and foreign-produced goods. First, the issue is critical to modeling behavior because PPP, if it were widely applicable, would provide a firm anchor for the formulation of expectations about the future or equilibrium value of the exchange rate. In addition, the extent of substitution between domestic and foreign-produced goods is central to the debate over effectiveness of exchange rate adjustments in reducing current account imbalances. The pessimists believe that exchange rate depreciations will have only a modest effect on trade flows, while imposing large costs in the form of worse terms of trade and increased inflation. Thus, they advocate more direct forms of intervention to limit imports or promote exports. At the opposite extreme is a group of economists who believe that the elasticities are so high that any required changes in real exchange rate are trivial. If that were true, a flexible exchange rate system would be unnecessary in that the changes in relative prices could be achieved with small variations in the domestic price level. These issues are examined empirically in chapters 4 and 5.

---

15. See, for example, Marston (1989).

Uncovered Interest Parity

Uncovered interest rate parity (UIP) is the condition that requires domestic and foreign bonds to earn equal rates of return after adjusting for any expected change in the exchange rate. Thus, the expected change in the exchange rate over a future period, T, is equal to the interest differential on domestic and foreign bonds over the same horizon:

$$(2\text{-}13) \qquad \Delta e_T^e = e - E(e_T) = i_T - i_T^*.$$

This condition can hold only if investors view domestic and foreign bonds as perfect substitutes in their portfolios.[16] UIP presupposes a complete integration of international capital markets, and it is the financial market equivalent of PPP in goods markets.

The degree of substitution between different types of financial assets has long been a point of contention in the analysis of domestic financial markets. It is well recognized that investors will desire to hold a diversified portfolio, but the current view is that at the margin the potential for substitution is very high: after adjusting for differences in maturity and changes in risk perceptions, the behavior of interest rates in these markets reflects near perfect substitution.

International capital markets have an added dimension, however, because investors have to concern themselves with the potential for changes in exchange rates, as well as variation in relative interest rates. Uncovered interest parity incorporates exchange rate effects by including any expected exchange rate change. The UIP condition asserts that national interest rates can differ only as a reflection of an expected change in the exchange rate.

As with PPP, the simple version of UIP, which equates the level of interest rates after adjusting for expected exchange rate changes, is too restrictive. Interest rate differentials can vary across markets and over time for a variety of reasons, including perceptions of risk, and still be consistent at the margin with perfect substitution in investors' portfolios. Thus, the UIP condition can be modified to include a risk premium and to allow investors' perception of risk to vary over time. What

---

16. It is useful to distinguish, as Frankel (1983) did, between capital mobility and substitutability. Capital mobility refers only to the institutional changes that permit investors to freely move funds between national capital markets and that thereby allow them to adjust their portfolios to desired levels. Perfect substitutes is a much stronger statement about investors' views of the distinction between domestic and foreign bonds.

is crucial for perfect substitution is that the premium must be independent of the relative quantities of the two assets.[17]

The degree of substitution between domestic and foreign bonds must be taken into account in modeling the international economy because financial capital is attracted to markets where high interest rates are indicative of a resource scarcity. It is the capital inflow that precipitates an exchange rate appreciation, and the subsequent inflow of real resources. In addition, most efforts to model the behavior of exchange rates assume that the potential for capital mobility is high and that UIP is a condition that can be assumed to hold in reality. The validity of the UIP assumption and the extent to which exchange rates respond to changes in relative interest rates are explored empirically in chapter 4.

Expenditure-Changing and Expenditure-Switching Policies

The two definitions of the current account in equations 2-1 and 2-6 seem to imply that there are two alternative approaches to altering the trade balance: one based on changing the relative price of domestic versus foreign goods, as highlighted by equation 2-1, and the other based on changing domestic demand by altering the domestic balance of saving and investment, as highlighted in equation 2-6. Harry Johnson popularized the terms "expenditure switching" and "expenditure reducing" to characterize these two approaches to eliminating a current account deficit. Examples of expenditure-switching policies are a domestic price deflation, a currency devaluation, or direct controls on trade using tariffs or quotas. A change in fiscal policy that lowers the level of domestic demand is an example of a expenditure-reducing action. Here, lower imports will constitute a part of the decline in total expenditures.[18]

There are some situations where it is useful to think of these two approaches as alternatives. A country in recession, for example, could promote an expansion by instituting an export subsidy, or it might choose to rely on fiscal expansion in the domestic economy.

In general, however, expenditure-switching and expenditure-changing policies should be viewed as complementary and equally necessary

17. Perfect substitution refers to the slope of the demand curve, a very high price elasticity. It is not necessary that the demand curves never shift.

18. The dichotomy is somewhat overdrawn because expenditure-changing policies will themselves induce some change in the relative price of domestic versus foreign goods, and measures directed at altering the relative price will have implications for domestic income and the demand for imports. See Johnson (1958).

aspects of a single adjustment process. This is particularly true for an economy that is at full employment with a substantial current account deficit.[19] Remember that the current account balance is equal to the balance of saving and investment; and it cannot be altered without adjusting the domestic balance, through expenditure-changing policies. For a deficit country operating at full employment, that means either lowering consumption (increased saving) or lower investment. The reduction in domestic spending is required in order to free up resources for export or to substitute for imports.

To prevent the reduction in domestic expenditures from translating into reduced output and employment, however, the resources that are freed up must be reallocated to foreign markets, through increased exports and reduced imports. It is true that the lower level of income will improve the trade balance by reducing imports, but such an approach will be very expensive in terms of unemployment. Most of the decline in domestic demand will fall on domestic producers. The preferred outcome would be to shift demand for the resources from the domestic to the foreign sector, leaving the total level of income and employment unchanged. That can only be accomplished, at a given level of foreign and domestic incomes, by altering the relative price of domestic versus foreign goods, through expenditure-switching policies.

Under ideal circumstances this whole process would occur quickly and automatically. The reduction in domestic demand would quickly lead to a small decline in domestic prices; and, if domestic and foreign goods are viewed as close substitutes, buyers in the global market would quickly switch from foreign to domestically produced goods. Expenditure switching policies would be a small part of the story, safely ignored while the focus is on the need to realign domestic saving and investment.

In practice the process encounters two problems. First, domestic wages and prices are quite sticky, and large changes in demand and employment are required to alter the average price level. Second, consumers are not quick to alter their preferences for domestic versus foreign goods, with the result that it takes so that substantial changes in relative prices to achieve a significant switching of expenditures.

Under a system of flexible exchange rates, however, the relative price of domestic and foreign goods is not determined solely by the path of

---

19. Clear expositions of the issues are provided by Corden (1986), Krugman and Baldwin (1987), and Krugman (1989).

the domestic price level in relation to that abroad, since changes in the nominal exchange rate will be equally important. Although, as emphasized earlier, governments cannot arbitrarily alter the exchange rate, they can influence it by changing relative interest rates. By adopting the appropriate mix of fiscal and monetary policies, governments can speed the process of adjustment with considerably less disruption to the domestic economy than would otherwise be necessary. The combination of a restrictive policy (fiscal restraint) and an easing of monetary policy (monetary ease), for example, can simultaneously free up domestic resources, and by inducing a decline in interest rates and the exchange rate speed the transfer of those resources into foreign markets.

3

International Trends in Saving and Investment

As noted at the outset of this discussion, the current account balance is defined as the difference between a nation's saving and its domestic investment. Countries that save less than they invest domestically must borrow from other countries—that is, they must import more than they export. Thus the large current account imbalances in the 1980s reflect altered relationships between domestic saving and investment. This chapter deals with the important changes in this area in industrial countries and the reasons behind them.

Consider, first, the case of the United States, whose falling national saving rate has generated considerable interest, primarily because of the change in the government budget deficit. Less attention has focused on the equally large decline in an already low rate of private saving, or on the fact that other industrial countries are experiencing similar declines in their rates of national saving. Whatever the cause of reduced saving, it would appear to be something that many countries have in common.

Furthermore, with the noteworthy exception of the United States, most industrial economies have experienced a larger decline in private investment rates than in private saving. In fact, since the first oil shock in 1973 many industrial countries have been plagued with an excess of private saving in relation to their investment needs. Efforts during the 1970s to restore the balance of private saving and investment by reducing real interest rates were unsuccessful, and governments, striving to maintain domestic employment, chose to absorb the surplus through larger budget deficits.[1] The alternative of shipping the excess saving

1. The fact that real interest rates were negative or very low in all these countries in the last half of the 1970s also argues against the notion that the large budget deficits were

abroad as a current account surplus was severely constrained by the need to find other economies willing to tolerate a current account deficit. At the time, the world economy was already under pressure to recycle the surpluses of the oil-producing countries. The pattern of large budget deficits represented a particularly sharp change for Japan and the European countries, which had relied on budget surpluses to augment private saving during the 1960s.

In the 1980s the United States experienced a dramatic shift toward increased consumption, both public and private, a consequent shortfall in saving, and the emergence of a large trade deficit. Other countries—particularly Japan and Germany—responded to the new American policy with a shift of their own: they eliminated their budget deficits and allowed their growing national saving to flow through to current account surpluses and offset the deficit of the United States. It is in this sense that today's current account imbalances are a reflection of underlying changes in saving and investment patterns.

The patterns of change in private rates of saving and investment are examined more fully in the following sections, beginning with a summary of some basic trends and statistical tests of alternative hypotheses that have been advanced to explain the declines in private saving and investment. It is important to identify the causes of the decline because the saving-investment framework cannot be a useful method of accounting for changes in current account balances, unless we are able to explain basic trends in domestic rates of saving and investment. And, if the current account is to be perceived as a reflection of domestic economic conditions, rather than a reflection of changes in the international economy, domestic rates of saving and investment should evolve in a fashion that is largely independent of international developments. The last parts of the chapter deal with the evolution of the private saving-investment (SI) balance and with the role of the public sector budget balance in augmenting or offsetting variations in the private balance. Throughout the chapter the analysis pays particular attention to the consistency of the empirical results across a set of fifteen industrial countries.[2]

---

crowding out private demand. Additional evidence of a general demand deficiency was provided by the pattern of rising rates of unemployment.

2. The basic national accounts data were obtained from the Organization for Economic Cooperation and Development and are based on the international System of National Accounts, which provides a uniform standard of definitions for comparing data from different countries. Some inconsistencies remain that are explained later in this chapter. The list of specific countries is shown in table 3-1. Some OECD countries are

Basic Trends in Saving and Investment

The annual data on which this study is based are drawn from the System of National Accounts (SNA) submitted by the individual member countries to the OECD for the period 1965 to 1990. The SNA eliminates most of the definitional differences that make it difficult to compare saving and investment on the basis of national sources. In contrast to the U.S. national accounts, for example, the SNA framework includes a capital account for the government sector, which makes it possible to distinguish between the saving and investment components of the government budget deficit. In addition, government enterprises are separated from the general government budget and are included with private business.

One significant problem that remains is that countries vary greatly in their treatment of capital consumption allowances (depreciation). Not only do they differ in their assumptions about the useful lives of capital, but in some cases they calculate capital consumption on the basis of historical costs, instead of replacement costs.[3] Although such differences make it difficult to compare levels of net saving or investment across countries, they are not of particular concern in the comparison of trends. Since capital consumption allowances have been a rising share of GDP, rates of net saving and investment show larger secular declines than those based on the gross data. The following analysis of saving and investment examines the behavior of both the net and gross series, although in most cases the choice has surprisingly little effect on the conclusions.

The international data further highlight the value of focusing on the saving of the private sector as whole rather than households. Household saving is not well-defined because it differs from private saving only by the exclusion of retained earnings of incorporated businesses and thus still includes all the internal financing of partnership and sole proprietorship businesses. Since the relative importance of incorporated businesses differs among countries, and since tax laws and financial structure substantially influence the extent of profit retention, house-

---

excluded from the analysis because a reliable full set of national accounts data was not available.

3. An adjustment was made to convert the Japanese estimate of capital consumption allowances from a historical cost basis to the standard current replacement cost basis. That change lowers the reported Japanese private saving rate in the 1970s and 1980s by 3 to 4 percentage points. For the details of that adjustment, see Hayashi (1986), pp. 201–10.

FIGURE 3-1. *Saving and Investment Rates, Four Industrial Economies, 1965–90[a]*

Percent of net domestic product

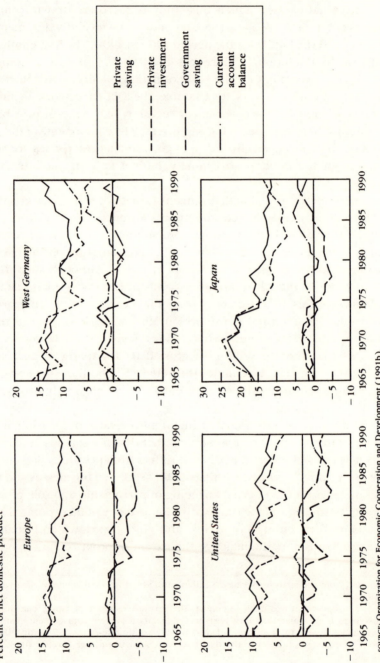

SOURCE: Organization for Economic Cooperation and Development (1991b).
a. Data aggregated using 1990 exchange rates.

hold saving rates are not truly comparable across countries. Moreover, it is often suggested that the owners of corporate equity should "pierce the corporate veil" and perceive retained earnings as the action of agents saving on their behalf, so that variations in corporate saving can be offset at the household level. These considerations suggest that the overall private saving rate is the more meaningful concept, and it is used throughout this chapter.

Data from the national accounts can be used to construct the relationship by which the current account balance is equal to domestic saving minus domestic investment. Saving and investment can be further divided between the government and private sectors. Because the distinction between government saving and investment is not critical to the present discussion of private-sector behavior, the two are combined into an overall measure of the budget deficit, namely, net lending.[4] Thus, the subsequent analysis is based on a simple accounting identity:

$$(3\text{-}1) \qquad\qquad CA = S_p - I_p + NL_g.$$

Private saving includes both the saving of individuals and the retained earnings of business firms. Private investment includes business investment in plant and equipment, inventory accumulation, and residential housing construction. In addition, investment and saving are measured on a net basis, by deducting capital consumption allowances. In the following analysis the data are expressed as a percentage of net domestic product to minimize the influence of simple increases in the scale of the data when measured over a long period of time.

The trends in the basic data are presented in figure 3-1, which shows the components of the identity for the United States, Japan, Germany, and an aggregate of eleven European countries.[5] The general nature of the decline in private rates of net saving and investment is evident in these figures, except in the case of private saving in Germany. Over the 1965–90 period private investment rates, measured in gross and net terms, fell in all of the countries in the sample, except the United Kingdom. The negative trend is statistically significant for fourteen of

---

4. This measure of net lending differs from the standard definition by excluding capital transfers that are allocated to the capital account in the SNA framework.

5. The aggregation was performed using nominal 1980 exchange rates. The private saving and investment data for Germany are limited to West Germany. The government budget deficit and the current account balance, however, include data on eastern Germany for 1990. The data for the other countries in the sample are shown in figure 3A-1 at the end of the chapter.

TABLE 3-1 *Private Net Saving and Investment, Share of Net Domestic Product by Country, Selected Periods, 1965–90*
Percent

Country	1965–72		1984–90		Change			Output growth rate		
	Private saving	Private investment	Private saving	Private investment	Private saving	Private investment	Balance[a]	1960–73	1973–90	Change
United States	10.5	8.7	7.4	5.6	-3.1	-3.1	0.0	4.0	2.6	-1.4
Canada	8.9	11.3	12.2	9.8	3.3	-1.5	4.8	5.4	3.3	-2.1
Japan	20.0	20.7	12.0	9.9	-8.0	-10.8	2.8	9.6	3.9	-5.7
Australia	10.9	13.9	4.4	10.3	-6.5	-3.6	-2.9	5.6	3.0	-2.6
Large European countries										
France	15.4	15.8	9.3	7.2	-6.1	-8.6	2.5	5.4	2.4	-3.0
Germany	13.4	13.7	11.6	7.4	-1.8	-6.3	4.5	4.4	2.1	-2.3
Italy	20.3	12.7	17.7	7.1	-2.6	-5.6	3.0	5.3	2.9	-2.4
United Kingdom	6.9	7.9	5.2	7.2	-1.7	-0.7	-1.0	3.2	1.9	-1.3
Small European countries										
Austria	11.5	14.4	12.1	10.9	0.6	-3.5	4.1	4.9	2.5	-2.4
Belgium	15.0	11.2	15.6	6.9	0.6	-4.3	4.9	4.9	2.2	-2.7
Denmark	9.7	15.4	6.5	9.5	-3.2	-5.9	2.7	4.3	1.8	-2.5
Finland	7.6	13.0	6.6	9.9	-1.0	-3.1	2.1	5.0	3.0	-2.0
Netherlands	15.8	15.6	16.1	8.7	0.3	-6.9	7.2	4.8	2.1	-2.7
Norway	7.0	13.3	4.0	9.8	-3.0	-3.5	0.5	4.3	3.4	-0.9
Sweden	4.4	10.2	4.1	6.7	-0.3	-3.5	3.2	4.1	1.8	-2.3
Total (15 countries)	12.6	12.1	9.6	7.3	-3.0	-4.8	1.8	4.8	2.7	-2.1

SOURCES: Organization for Economic Cooperation and Development (1991b) and author's calculations as explained in the text.
a. Defined as private saving minus private investment.

the fifteen countries in the case of net investment and ten countries for gross investment. Evidence of a decline in private saving rates is less clear-cut. Rates of net saving have moved down in twelve countries; but gross saving rates show no consistent trend, rising in eight countries and falling in seven.

The reduction in the government balance is more striking. During the 1960s, government saving typically exceeded government investment; and, with the notable exception of the United States, governments made a positive contribution to the financing of private capital formation. After 1973, most governments experienced large budget deficits that continued on into the 1980s. Several countries, again with the exception of the United States, reduced their budget deficits or even shifted back to a surplus in the mid-1980s. Finally, prior to 1980 changes in the balance of private saving and investment tended to be absorbed in changes in the government budget balance, rather than the current account. That pattern is somewhat less evident in the 1980s.

An alternative summary of the long-run trends is shown in table 3-1. Average rates of private net saving and investment are shown for fifteen OECD countries between two periods, 1965–72 and 1984–90. They represent approximately 95 percent of OECD output as a whole. The periods were chosen to highlight the differences that began to emerge after 1973 and to eliminate as much as possible the short-run influence of the two large recessions of 1974–75 and 1980–82. The most striking aspect of table 3-1 is the extent of general decline in the rates of both private saving and investment. On the aggregate, the rate of private saving has fallen by 3 percentage points of net domestic product, and net investment is down by nearly 5 percentage points. The fall in the net investment rate since 1973 equals nearly 11 percent of NDP for Japan and averages more than 5 percentage points in Western Europe. The reduction in private saving rates is consistently less than that in investment, the result being a strong shift toward a surplus of private saving over private investment. The exceptions are Australia, the United Kingdom, and the United States, where the fall in the rate of saving has equaled or surpassed the drop in investment. The behavior of the private sector alone suggests that most industrial countries should have had large current account surpluses in the 1980s.

It is important, however, to recognize which aspect of this change in the saving-investment balance was a surprise from an economic perspective. Standard neoclassical growth theory emphasizes the relationship between the stock of capital and the level of output, a flow variable.

If relative prices and the capital intensity of technological change do not vary, the capital-output ratio, β, is expected to be constant and independent of the level of output. And if investment is interpreted as an adjustment to a desired capital stock, the share of net investment in output should be proportionate to the rate of output growth:

$$(3-2) \qquad\qquad K = \beta Y,$$

$$(3-3) \qquad\qquad K - K_{-1} = \beta(y - Y_{-1}),$$

$$(3-4) \qquad\qquad I/Y = \beta \Delta Y/Y.$$

Similarly, according to the life cycle hypothesis (LCH), the wealth-income ratio (α) is invariant to the level of income:[6]

$$(3-5) \qquad\qquad W = \alpha Y,$$

$$(3-6) \qquad\qquad W - W_{-1} = \alpha(Y - Y_{-1}),$$

$$(3-7) \qquad\qquad S/Y = \alpha \Delta Y/Y.$$

Thus, by the same logic that relates investment to the change in output, the saving rate is also a positive function of the rate of income growth.

As shown in the far right column of table 3-1, all the industrial countries have experienced a substantial reduction in economic growth since 1973, which provides a potentially straightforward explanation for the decline in their rates of private saving and investment. The decline in economic growth is particularly large for Japan and several European countries, exceeding 50 percent of the pre-1973 rate.

It is possible to adjust for differences in rates of income growth and obtain estimates of the underlying wealth-income, α, and capital-output, β, ratios for each of the two subperiods by dividing the growth rate into the saving and investment rates, respectively. These calculations are shown in table 3-2. Interestingly enough, the adjustment for differences in income growth substantially changes the relative rankings of the countries: the U.S. rate of wealth accumulation is no longer particularly low in relation to income, and Japan's is not high. Because there is a strong positive correlation across countries between rates of

---

6. For a recent statement of this view, see Modigliani (1986), p. 301. In the version of the life cycle hypothesis developed by Modigliani and others, however, the wealth-income ratio, although independent of the level of income, is expected to vary inversely with the rate of income growth. This hypothesized effect is small, but it is enough to imply that the positive effect of economic growth on the saving rate is dampened in relation to that for the investment rate.

TABLE 3-2. *Implied Ratios of Wealth to Income and Capital to Output Ratios, Fifteen OECD Countries, 1965–72, 1984–90*

Country	Implied wealth-income ratio			Implied capital-output ratio		
	1965–72	1984–90	Change	1965–72	1984–90	Change
United States	2.6	2.8	0.2	2.2	2.2	0.0
Canada	1.6	3.7	2.1	2.1	3.0	0.9
Japan	2.1	3.1	1.0	2.2	2.5	0.3
Australia	1.9	1.5	−0.4	2.5	3.4	0.9
Large European countries						
France	2.9	3.9	1.0	2.9	3.0	0.1
Germany	3.0	5.5	2.5	3.1	3.5	0.4
Italy	3.8	6.1	2.3	2.4	2.4	0.0
United Kingdom	2.2	2.7	0.5	2.5	3.8	1.3
Small European countries						
Austria	2.3	4.8	2.5	2.9	4.4	1.5
Belgium	3.1	7.1	4.0	2.3	3.1	0.8
Denmark	2.3	3.6	1.3	3.6	5.3	1.7
Finland	1.5	2.2	0.7	2.6	3.3	0.7
Netherlands	3.3	7.7	4.4	3.3	4.1	0.8
Norway	1.6	1.2	−0.4	3.1	2.9	−0.2
Sweden	1.1	2.3	1.2	2.5	3.7	1.2

SOURCES: Table 3-1 and author's calculations as explained in the text.

income growth and rates of saving and investment, the adjustment clearly reduces the dispersion of both saving and investment rates.

A comparison of the pre- and post-1973 periods, however, indicates that the reductions in the rates of saving and investment are both less than proportionate to the decline in output growth, as is evident from the consistent increase in the estimated values of α and β after 1973. The exceptions are Australia and Norway for saving and the United States and Norway for investment. In addition, the estimated capital-output ratios (investment) are far more stable than the estimated wealth-income ratio (saving).

The declines in rates of private saving and investment therefore seem less unusual when the role of income growth is taken into account. Given the slowdown in economic growth, declines in rates of private saving and investment are not a surprise. In fact, most industrial countries are accumulating private wealth and physical capital at a more rapid pace in relation to the growth in their incomes than they did in the past. Furthermore, rates of private saving have fared better than rates of investment, considering that the increase in the wealth-income ratio is generally larger than for physical capital.

Alternative Explanations of Private Saving

The above framework overlooks a large number of factors stressed in the literature on saving behavior. Most empirical work on saving behavior has been undertaken in the context of the life cycle model. Individuals are assumed to maximize the present value of their lifetime utility, subject to a budget constraint that is equal to their current net worth plus the present value of the labor income that they expect to earn over their remaining worklife. Within this framework, variations in aggregate private saving should result primarily from changes in demographics, income growth, interest rates and inflation, and, perhaps, changes in public sector budget deficits that shift tax burdens to future generations. These issues are explored further in the following sections, but the results of the empirical analysis serve mainly to reinforce the point that income growth is the principal determinant of observed changes in saving rates.

Demographics

Few time-series studies of consumption behavior have paid much attention to changes in the age structure of the population. Because these changes occur very gradually, their influence is difficult to detect. Yet, the age composition of the population is thought to be an important component of life cycle models of aggregate saving behavior. More people have become interested in the role of demographic change in recent years because it is alleged that the large increases in the elderly population of most industrial countries over the next several decades will cause drastic reductions in the rates of private saving. Some studies are predicting that Japan, for example, will join the United States by the turn of the century and become a net seller of its assets internationally to support its level of consumption.[7] Others argue that demographic factors will contribute to substantial increases in the U.S. saving rate as the baby-boom generation matures.

---

7. The potential for sharply lower rates of future saving as a result of an increase in the proportion of retirees in the population is stressed in Heller (1989). Horioka (1989a, 1989b), for example, projects negative private saving rates for Japan early in the twenty-first century.

TABLE 3-3. *Cross-National Estimates of the Influence of Demographics on Private Saving, Selected Periods, 1960–85*

1. Modigliani-Sterling (1962–73)

   $S = 2.3 G1 - 0.48 AGE - 0.11 DEP + 0.27 CHPR - 0.09 B/E + 0.05$

      (7.6)   (4.0)   (1.2)   (2.7)   (2.0)

                                                  $SEE = 0.02$

                                                    $n = 21$

2. Feldstein (1960–75)

   $S = 5.24 G2 - 1.21 AGE - 0.77 DEP - 0.54 LPAGED - 0.37 B/E + 0.92$

      (3.9)   (2.7)   (3.8)   (2.0)   (2.8)

                                                  $SEE = 0.02$

                                                    $n = 12$

3. Horioka (1975–84)

   $S = 0.79 G1 - 1.09 AGE - 0.43 DEP - 0.15 LPAGED + 1140.1 IPCY + 0.46$

      (0.5)   (2.4)   (1.7)   (1.0)   (2.9)

                                                  $SEE = $ n.a.

                                                    $n = 21$

4. Bosworth (1962–73, 1976–85)

   $S = 1.73 G2 - 0.77 AGED - 0.36 DEP - 0.22 LPAGED + 0.48$

      (3.2)   (2.9)   (3.1)   (2.2)

                                                  $SEE = 0.04$

                                                    $n = 30$

SOURCES: Feldstein (1980); Modigliani and Sterling (1980); Horioka (1989); and author's calculations. T-statistics are in parentheses.

$G1$ is the annual growth of real per capita disposable income. $G2$ is the annual growth of real private disposable income. AGE is the ratio of retired persons over 65 years of age to persons between ages 20 and 65. In the case of Horioka, the ratio includes all persons over 65. DEP is the ratio of persons under 20 years to persons between ages 20 and 65 (for Modigliani-Sterling, the denominator of AGE and DEP is the male population, aged 20 to 65). $LPAGED$ is the labor-force participation rate of males aged 65 and over. $CHPR$ is the difference of male participation rate between ages 25 and 55 and 65+ expressed as a ratio to the former. B/E is the benefit replacement rate (ratio to earnings) for public pension programs. $IPCY$ is the reciprocal of per capita income (U.S. dollars).

Several cross-national studies have concluded that differences in the age structure account for a significant portion of the international variation in the level of private saving rates. Three of the more detailed studies in this area—by Martin Feldstein, Franco Modigliani and A. Sterling, and Charles Horioka—are summarized in table 3-3. These authors used a similar underlying model, in which the humped characteristic of the age profile of saving is captured by including the proportions of the population that are young or retired.[8] They averaged private saving rates over several years to eliminate cyclical influences and related the international variations in saving to differences in rates of income growth, the demographic structure of the population, and the generosity of public social insurance programs. Countries with a

8. Modigliani (1970).

high ratio of dependents (children and retired individuals) in relation to the population of working age were found to have relatively low saving rates. Furthermore, an increase in the proportion of the male population over age 65 that is retired was found to be an effective proxy for changes in the expected length of the retirement period, which should raise the rate of saving during the working years.

In reestimating the equations of Feldstein and of Modigliani and Sterling, I found that subsequent data revisions weaken their original conclusions—particularly, with respect to the influence of social security programs. In addition, the estimated parameters are highly sensitive to the specific list of countries that are included in the analysis and the data period. The use of data from later years sharply reduces the explanatory role of differences in income growth. By combining data for the 1960–72 and 1976–86 periods, however, it is possible to obtain similar results for the demographic variables (equation 4 in table 3-3).[9]

Although the studies vary in the absolute magnitude of the coefficients on the demographic variables, they agree on the sign of the individual coefficients and the relative importance of the young versus the elderly. An increase in the proportion of the population under age 20 reduces the private saving rate by about half as much as an equivalent increase in the proportion that is retired.

The coefficients on the three demographic variables in equation 4, table 3-3, are used to compute a time-series index of demographic effects for each country.[10] Surprisingly, these indexes imply that demographic changes should have led to dramatically higher private saving rates over the past two decades, with the magnitude of the change differing widely among the countries of the sample. Column one of table 3-4 presents the same change in the private saving rate between 1965–72 and 1984–87 that was shown in table 3-3. The net contribution of demographic change is shown in column 2. The effect of demographic changes on saving is negative only for Sweden.

---

9. Horioka's study differs primarily in his use of the number of persons over age 65, rather than the number of retired elderly. In addition, I obtained more significant results when I did not weight the sample observations by the relative size of each country's GNP, as was done in the other studies.

10. The basic results do not particularly depend on the choice of a specific equation in table 3-3 to construct the index because the relative magnitudes of the demographic coefficients are very similar. Indexes based on the first three equations in this table show the same pattern as reported in table 3-4, except that the magnitude of change is even larger. The data on the demographic composition of the population over the 1965–90 period were obtained primarily from OECD (1989b).

TABLE 3-4. *Measures of the Effect of Demographics on Changes in Private Saving Rate, by Country, 1965–72, 1984–90*
Percent of net domestic product

Country	Actual change in saving rate	Predicted change	
		Equation 4	Equation 4'
United States	− 3.1	6.5	4.4
Canada	3.3	9.6	6.9
Japan	− 8.0	3.4	0.1
Australia	− 6.5	5.6	2.4
Large European countries			
France	− 6.1	5.9	2.1
Germany	− 1.8	5.0	1.8
Italy	− 2.6	1.1	− 1.1
United Kingdom	− 1.7	1.9	− 1.0
Small European countries			
Austria	0.6	4.6	3.0
Belgium	0.6	a	a
Denmark	− 3.2	2.5	− 0.3
Finland	− 1.0	3.8	− 2.6
Netherlands	0.3	8.4	5.6
Norway	− 3.0	a	a
Sweden	− 0.3	− 0.8	− 5.0

SOURCE: Tables 3-1 and 3-3 and author's calculations as explained in the text.
a. Not included in regression.

The reason for the positive contribution of demographic change is simple. A large decline in the number of young people has offset the rise in the proportion of the population that is retired. In addition, an increased propensity to retire, a proxy for a longer expected period of retirement, has exerted a substantial positive effect on the private saving rate of all the countries. In fact, it is the change in the retirement rate, not the age distribution, that dominates the change in the indexes. This is shown in column three of table 3-4, which excludes the contribution of the retirement rate variable. The most surprising aspect of table 3-3 is the large magnitude of the implied change. Yet, the coefficients used to compute the indexes are smaller than those of the earlier studies.

In the following analysis of the time-series data, these indexes are used to represent the net contribution of demographic changes. The use of a single index, based on weights from the cross-sectional analysis, is designed to overcome some of the problems of collinearity between the various components of demographic change that have plagued earlier studies.

Income Growth

Substantial confusion surrounds the relationship between saving and income growth. A positive effect of income growth on the aggregate saving rate is often cited as a key conclusion of the life cycle model and is used to account for international differences in the level of private saving rates.[11] That conclusion is obtained as an implication of aggregation, however, not the underlying behavior of individual households. The aggregate saving rate is a weighted average of the saving rates of individual age cohorts:

$$(3\text{-}8) \qquad S = \sum w_i \cdot y_i \cdot s_i \qquad \text{for } i = 1, n,$$

where S = the overall average saving rate, s_i = the saving rate of the ith age group, w_i = proportion of household heads in the ith age group, and y_i = ratio of average income in the ith group to the overall average.

Within the behavioral model used by Modigliani, income growth is assumed to have no effect on the saving rate of any individual age cohort. Instead, the hypothesized positive correlation is a consequence of the fact that an increased rate of income growth, whether from increases in population or productivity, raises the incomes of workers (savers) in relation to the retired (dissavers), changing the weights attached to the saving rate of individual age cohorts through the aggregation process outlined in equation 3-8.

The generality of the conclusion, however, was challenged by James Tobin and M. J. Farrell, who noted that it depended on the assumption that each individual does not anticipate future income changes—static expectations—and that dissaving occurs only in retirement.[12] Within the life cycle model, current consumption depends on an individual's expected lifetime resources, which consist of current nonhuman wealth plus the present value of expected future wage income. Modigliani's version of the life cycle model assumed that individuals would not revise their estimates of future wage income in response to variations in aggregate productivity growth.

---

11. The argument is laid out in Modigliani (1966) and empirical support is provided in Modigliani (1970, 1980) and Feldstein (1980).
12. Tobin (1967) and Farrell (1970).

Alternatively, if consumers are forward looking, expectations of higher future wage growth will raise the present value of lifetime resources and lead to an increase in current consumption. That is, expectations of higher income growth should reduce saving within age cohorts, offsetting the "among-cohort" effect introduced through the aggregation of groups with different saving rates. Saving is postponed until it is less costly in terms of forgone consumption. The effect should be particularly pronounced for young households, for whom the present value of future wage income is a large proportion of lifetime resources.

Thus, income growth will affect the private saving rate through two channels: its effect on the expectations of individual households, and its effect on the aggregation process. At the level of individual households, saving should be negatively related to the expected rate of income growth. On the other hand, aggregation across households, in which wage earners are savers and the retired are dissavers, implies a positive relationship between the aggregate saving rate and income growth. In simulation models that incorporate the two effects, Tobin and Farrell both found that the within-cohort effect dominated, producing a negative relationship between income growth and aggregate saving.[13]

The impact of income growth on saving rates is further complicated by the positive short-run correlation that will exist between contemporaneous measures of income and saving simply because unanticipated changes in income will be largely absorbed by changes in saving rather than consumption. In the following analysis the rate of growth of income in the current period is included as a reflection of the transitory component, while a longer-moving average of income growth is used to measure the influence of changes in expected future income. One version used a centered moving average to give some weight to actual future developments, but that was no better than an average of income growth over the past four years, which is reported in the final version.

Wealth

The basic life cycle model suggests that the net wealth of the private sector and variations in its value due to capital gains and losses should

---

13. Similar conclusions are implied by the formulation of the life cycle model used by Summers (1981).

be a determinant of saving. However, measures of private wealth are only available for a few of the countries in the sample. A rough measure can be constructed using the relationship in which wealth is the cumulative sum of past saving plus capital gains (CG):

$$(3-9) \qquad W_t = W_{t-1} + Sp_t + CG_t.$$

The importance of capital gains and losses can be minimized by measuring equation 3-9 in real terms, cumulating past saving in constant 1980 prices. An initial starting value for the stock of wealth was chosen so that the average wealth-income ratio of the 1965–72 period was the same as that implied by the ratio of the flow data, as shown in table 3-2. At the level of the total private sector, real capital gains and losses are by and large limited to variations in real estate and share prices, and the effect of inflation on the real value of the public debt. Other forms of capital gains and losses should cancel in the process of aggregation. An index of corporate share prices, deflated by the consumption price index, is included in the regressions to account for real capital gains or losses arising from changes in share prices. No measure of real estate prices was available. The role of the public debt is discussed in the following section.

Inflation and Interest Rates

The rate of price inflation could affect private saving through three channels. First, it is an element of the real rate of interest; an increased rate of inflation, in the presence of an unchanged nominal interest rate, provides an incentive for individuals to lower their rate of saving. The two components of the real rate may not exert equal offsetting effects on saving, however, if individuals are subject to liquidity constraints or if they are limited in their ability to hedge their wealth portfolio against inflation risks. Thus, price inflation and the nominal interest rate are often viewed as separate determinants of saving.

Second, it has been suggested that higher rates of inflation may translate into greater uncertainty about the future and thus increased precautionary saving, providing an additional reason for viewing it as a separate influence on saving.

Third, in measuring income the system of national accounts does not adjust for the component of nominal interest payments that simply compensates bondholders for the inflation-induced decline in the real value of their assets. Thus, the national accounts overstate the income and saving of creditors and understate that of debtors by an amount that varies directly with the rate of inflation.[14] Within a closed economy these revaluation effects alter the allocation of income and saving among sectors without changing the national total. Ignoring changes in the net foreign balance, a direct measure of the correction for the private sector as a whole can be introduced by multiplying the rate of inflation by the outstanding net financial liabilities of government.[15] Subtracting this inflation component of interest income from both private saving and private sector income yields an alternative inflation-adjusted saving rate.

The adjustment has a highly variable effect on private saving rates. Inflation was more pronounced in the 1970s than in the 1980s, and it reached particularly high levels in 1974−75. Thus, several countries with high levels of government indebtedness and high inflation rates, notably the United Kingdom and Italy, show sharp declines in the adjusted measure of the private saving rate in 1974−75 with a recovery in the 1980s when inflation receded. In contrast, the governments of Japan and Germany had positive net asset positions in the mid-1970s, and the adjustment raises the estimate of the private saving rate during the same period. For most countries the range of variation in the adjustment over the 1965−90 period is 2−4 percent of GDP, but for the United Kingdom and Italy it amounts to 11 and 8 percent of GDP, respectively.

The long-term government bond rate, available from the OECD, is used as a measure of the nominal return on savings; and expected inflation is measured with a three-year weighted average of changes in the consumer price deflator—with weights of 0.5, 0.3, and 0.2. Not enough data were available to adjust for variations in tax rates.

Ricardo-Barro Equivalence

If individuals undertake actions to neutralize the effects of variations in public saving in their own intertemporal spending plans and those of future generations, the national saving rate would be the appropriate measure of private intentions.[16] Although the underlying assumptions

14. Hill (1984) discusses and provides references pertaining to the importance of the changes in the real value of monetary assets due to inflation.
15. No attempt is made to correct for the effects of exchange rates and inflation in other countries on the real value of foreign assets and liabilities.
16. See Barro (1974). An evaluation of the Ricardo-Barro equivalence theorem is provided in Bernheim (1987).

of the theorem may seem quite far-fetched, we can test for its potential relevance by including the public sector saving rate as a potential determinant of the private saving rate.

Empirical Results

Although the following model is loosely specified, it incorporates empirical measures of the major factors believed to influence the private saving rate.

$$(3\text{-}10) \qquad rs_p = \alpha_0 + \beta_1 r + \beta_2 p + \beta_3 A + \beta_4 cp + \beta_5 dy + \beta_6 demo + \beta_7 rs_g,$$

where rs_p = private saving as a percentage of private disposable income; r = real interest rate; p = rate of inflation; A = private net worth as a percent of disposable income; cp = index of corporate equity prices, divided by disposable income; dy = percentage change of per capita real private disposable income (lagged effects are incorporated using a second degree polynomial extending over five years); $demo$ = index of demographic changes; and rs_g = government saving as a percentage of private disposable income.

This relationship is far too complex to estimate reliably on the basis of the data available for any one country. Reasonably accurate information on private saving rates are available for most countries only for the period since 1960. After allowing for lags, the number of observations was limited to about twenty-five years. In some cases it would be possible to increase the number of observations by using quarterly data, but that does not really resolve the problem when the focus of the analysis is on the longer-term fluctuations in saving behavior.[17]

Instead, the data were examined using two different methods of analysis. First, regressions were estimated for each of the countries in the sample in a process that excluded variables that were clearly statistically insignificant. At this stage, the primary objective was to determine the extent of uniformity in the structure of the saving relationship across countries and to identify those variables that were statistically significant in a majority of countries. Second, the data were pooled in

---

17. The limited number of observations prohibited the use of some recently popular methods of statistical analysis, such as cointegration techniques. The data have been scaled by income, however, to minimize the influence of divergent trends. In addition, a time trend was included at various stages of the analysis to ensure that the conclusions were not unduly influenced by trend factors.

a single large regression in which coefficients were constrained to be fixed across countries, so that there were a large number of observations in relation to the number of parameters to be estimated.

INDIVIDUAL COUNTRIES. The regressions for each country were initially estimated for the period 1965–90 using four measures of the private saving rate: gross and net saving, both with and without the adjustment to exclude the inflation component of government interest payments. The differences in the results between the net and gross measures were not substantial, but the gross saving rates had slightly smaller residual errors and less cyclical variability. The inflation adjustment to interest income produced substantially larger variations in the private saving rate, and that variability carried over to the estimated residual errors.[18] Thus, detailed results for individual countries are reported only for the conventional measure of the gross saving rate. Furthermore, because of the large number of potential regressors, individual variables were excluded from the reported regression when the coefficients were clearly of little statistical significance.

The measures of private wealth and the stock price index were excluded from all the reported regressions. The stock price index was statistically insignificant for all the countries; and the wealth-income ratio was consistently small. The failure of the wealth variables may be due to problems in identifying real capital gains and losses other than those on corporate stock. Official measures of private wealth are available for two countries, Japan and the United States, where the variation in real capital gains has been particularly large. Those measures performed equally poorly. Capital gains were widely blamed for the lower rates of saving in the United States and the United Kingdom during the 1980s; but the difficulty with that suggestion is that no correlation was detected in earlier periods. The argument that capital gains can account for the decline in saving rates seems particularly overstated when one reflects on the experience of Japan, where real capital gains have been phenomenal.[19]

---

18. An alternative approach to test for the influence of the inflation adjustment was to include the adjustment itself as an explanatory variable in a regression using the conventional definition of saving. This yielded a coefficient that differed significantly from zero for four countries, but it was perverse in sign and significant for four other countries.

19. The ratio of wealth to disposable income in the household sector of Japan rose from 4.1 in 1975 to 8.5 in 1990.

The empirical results are summarized in table 3-5.[20] The most uniform finding is the consistently positive relationship between saving rates and income growth. Furthermore, the income term seems to reflect something more than just transitory income movements, because the average growth over the preceding four years was significant in ten of the countries. The coefficients on income growth (including both the current and lagged changes) are highly variable, however, ranging from 0.4 to 1.8; and they are far below the average wealth-income ratios reported in table 3-2, which are clustered about 3.0.

The influence of other variables appears to vary substantially across countries. Demographics plays a statistically significant role in five of the thirteen countries for which demographic data were available, but the coefficients vary widely from the value of unity that would be expected if the results were to be fully consistent with the cross-national regressions of table 3-3. The coefficients are particularly large for Japan and Denmark.[21] In other countries the coefficients were perverse in sign or very close to zero.

Positive coefficients on interest rates were obtained for four countries, but they were statistically significant in only two cases. Inflation had a consistent positive net effect on saving, rather than the negative sign that would be expected if its dominant effect was operating through a real interest rate mechanism. The positive coefficient on the inflation rate would appear to support the adjusted measure of private saving that excluded the inflation component of interest income. Surprisingly, the positive coefficient persisted in equations using the adjusted saving measure.

Six countries showed evidence of a negative correlation between variations in government and private saving rates. The coefficient was consistently less than the value of unity implied by the extreme version of ultrarationality, but it does suggest some trade-off between government and private saving. However, it may be that the correlation reflects

20. Equations are not reported for Norway and the Netherlands because no meaningful results could be obtained. It would appear that part of the variability in private saving of these two countries is associated with earnings from energy exports. The third large energy producer, the United Kingdom, also displays a significant correlation between private saving and net energy exports.

21. Horioka (1989b) too finds evidence of a major role for demographics in the time-series data of Japan. His estimates are based on simple ratios of the young and the elderly, excluding any role for the retirement rate. However, his construction led to the inference that demographic trends had reduced the saving rate in the 1970–90 period. The inference here is that demographic changes increased the saving rate.

common cyclical influences on both variables or correlated measurement errors, because the government saving rate was seldom significant if it was lagged by one period.

Nearly all the equations contain a highly significant coefficient on a simple time trend. The trend term was included only if it improved or left unaffected the significance of other variables in the regression, but its presence is indicative of some unspecified influence on private saving rates. The coefficient is most frequently negative and surprisingly large.[22]

The regressions account for a substantial proportion of the variation in private saving rates in most countries; hence, the residual errors are quite small. The overall goodness of fit, however, is achieved at the cost of considerable variation in the structure of the relationship across countries. In fact, the coefficient estimates were more sensitive to variations in specification than is implied by reporting a single set of estimates.

The results reported in table 3-5 were extended to test two additional hypotheses. First, it is possible that the foreign sector has a direct impact on domestic saving rates operating through effects on the terms of trade. A worsening of the terms of trade increases the cost of imported consumption goods. This terms-of-trade factor, called the Laursen-Metzler-Harberger effect, may lead consumers to reduce their saving to maintain their living standards. This possibility was tested by including the ratio of export to import prices in the saving equations. A statistically significant positive coefficient was obtained only for Italy and Denmark.

Second, the emphasis on private saving rates assumes that households see through the "corporate veil" in adjusting for saving undertaken within corporate enterprises. This assumption can be tested directly for nine countries for which estimates of saving by the household sector were available. The equations were reestimated with the household saving rate as the dependent variable and including the corporate component of saving on the right-hand side of the regression. If households

---

22. One aspect that is not addressed relates to the potential influence of financial liberalization. Throughout the 1980s many countries liberalized the access of households to the mortgage market. If households were previously constrained in borrowing against real estate, the liberalization may have allowed a transition to a higher debt-asset ratio, with some of the proceeds being used to finance consumption. This process may have been important in Sweden, for example, where the household saving rate was negative in the last half of the 1980s.

TABLE 3-5. *Regression Estimates for Private Gross Saving Rates, 1965–90*

Country	Demo-graphics	Income growth, short-run	Income growth, lagged	Inflation	Interest rates	Government saving	Time trend	R^2	Standard error	Durbin-Watson
United States	0.40 (1.9)	0.27 (6.2)	0.29 (3.5)	0.53 (7.0)	a	-0.19 (3.9)	-0.26 (3.8)	0.96	0.3	2.3
Canada	a	0.21 (3.9)	0.20 (3.5)	0.59 (6.8)	0.19 (1.6)	-0.28 (5.4)	a	0.91	0.7	0.8
Japan	2.12 (10.4)	0.28 (8.8)	0.67 (13.4)	0.39 (6.9)	a	a	-0.25 (4.5)	0.97	0.5	2.1
Australia	a	0.45 (7.9)	0.43 (3.5)	0.44 (8.4)	a	a	-0.14 (5.3)	0.90	0.8	1.1
Large European countries										
France	a	0.57 (9.9)	1.21 (15.6)	0.53 (12.1)	a	a	a	0.94	0.5	1.8
Germany	0.28 (2.9)	0.31 (5.3)	0.66 (6.0)	a	0.24 (1.1)	a	a	0.84	0.7	0.7
United Kingdom[b]	a	0.27 (3.6)	a	a	0.52 (3.0)	-0.38 (4.1)	-0.27 (5.5)	0.84	1.1	1.4

Italy	0.54 (2.0)	0.41 (7.1)	0.34 (3.1)	0.20 (5.7)	a	−0.50 (5.1)	−0.22 (6.8)	0.93	0.5	1.5

Small European countries

Austria	a	0.32 (5.1)	0.72 (6.5)	0.29 (2.6)	0.71 (4.7)		0.12 (6.3)	0.89	0.5	2.5
Belgium	a	0.36 (6.0)	0.56 (6.3)	0.16 (2.1)	a		0.08 (4.0)	0.86	0.6	2.2
Denmark	1.57 (1.2)	0.33 (3.1)	a	0.30 (1.3)	a	−0.14 (1.9)	−0.27 (1.8)	0.57	1.5	1.0
Finland	0.37 (3.4)	0.27 (4.6)	0.47 (4.2)	a	a	a	0.14 (3.7)	0.81	1.2	1.7
Sweden	a	0.33 (4.0)	0.50 (2.8)	a	a	−0.34 (9.7)	−0.08 (2.2)	0.89	0.9	1.2

SOURCE: Author's calculations as explained in the text. T-statistics are in parentheses.
a. Variables excluded from regression.
b. The equation for the United Kingdom includes net exports of energy as a percentage of net national product and the interest rate is measured in nominal terms.

do take into account corporate saving, the coefficient on corporate saving should be negative and close to unity. The resulting coefficients together with their standard errors were as follows:

Country	Coefficient		Country	Coefficient	
United States	−0.98	(0.20)	United Kingdom	−0.23	(0.19)
Japan	−0.65	(0.14)	Belgium	−1.04	(0.24)
Canada	−0.74	(0.15)	Finland	−0.78	(0.29)
France	−0.95	(0.24)	Sweden	−0.59	(0.14)
Germany	−0.78	(0.12)			

The hypothesis that households do adjust for corporate saving can be strongly rejected only for the United Kingdom, Japan, and Sweden. The coefficients were not statistically different from unity for six of the nine countries.

POOLED REGRESSIONS. Pooling the data into a single regression greatly increases the number of observations, but it requires uniform coefficients on the various determinants of saving behavior across all the countries. Table 3-6 shows the results for the twelve countries for which all the data were available for 1965 to 1990, a total of 312 observations. Shift terms were included to allow for differences in saving rates that are specific to each country.

The first column reports the results of estimating equation 3-10 using the unadjusted measure of the gross private saving rate. In contrast to the regressions for individual countries, most of the coefficients are statistically significant with the expected sign. The income growth terms are also highly significant, although the cumulative magnitude of the effect, 0.48, is smaller than in the equations for the individual countries. In part, this is due to the presence of the wealth variable, which is now statistically significant. If it were excluded, the sum of the coefficients on income growth would rise to 0.66. Share prices, however, still show no important correlation with saving. Demographic changes continue to exert only a small effect on saving—the coefficient is about one-tenth the size of that found in the cross-sectional analysis. The real interest rate is statistically significant but with a negative sign. There also continues to be a highly significant, but small, negative correlation with the government saving rate. One surprise is the insignificant role of the inflation rate, a variable that appeared in several of the regressions for individual countries. Finally, the terms of trade have a positive and significant coefficient. This implies that a 10 percent

TABLE 3-6. *Pooled Regression Estimates for Measures of Private Saving Rates, 1965–90*

Variable	Gross saving	Adjusted gross[a]	Net saving	Adjusted net[a]	Modified gross
Income growth					
Current	0.21	0.16	0.29	0.22	0.18
	(6.4)	(4.4)	(7.1)	(5.0)	(6.5)
Lagged one year	0.15	0.10	0.22	0.14	0.14
	(5.0)	(2.8)	(5.6)	(3.4)	(5.1)
Lagged two years	0.09	0.06	0.13	0.09	0.08
	(3.3)	(1.8)	(3.8)	(2.3)	(3.1)
Lagged three years	0.02	−0.01	0.04	−0.003	b
	(0.8)	(0.3)	(1.2)	(0.1)	
Interest rates	−0.14	−0.16	−0.21	−0.24	−0.19
	(2.8)	(2.8)	(3.3)	(3.7)	(4.9)
Inflation	0.07	−0.05	−0.06	−0.24	b
	(1.4)	(0.9)	(0.8)	(3.3)	
Demographics	0.13	0.18	0.17	0.24	0.16
	(2.6)	(3.1)	(2.7)	(3.6)	(3.9)
Government saving	−0.25	−0.24	−0.33	−0.32	−0.28
	(9.6)	(8.3)	(10.1)	(9.2)	(12.8)
Terms of trade	2.72	4.05	5.90	7.83	2.45
	(3.5)	(4.6)	(6.1)	(7.6)	(3.3)
Wealth	−1.64	−3.51	−2.03	−4.57	−1.83
	(3.4)	(6.6)	(3.4)	(7.2)	(5.4)
Stock prices	−0.03	0.08	−0.28	−0.14	b
	(0.4)	(0.9)	(2.9)	(1.3)	
Time trend	0.02	0.07	−0.10	−0.04	b
	(0.9)	(2.8)	(4.0)	(1.6)	
Standard error	1.33	1.50	1.66	1.77	1.34

SOURCE: Author's calculations as explained in the text. T-statistics are in parentheses.
a. Adjusted for effects of inflation.
b. Variables excluded from regression.

increase in the terms of trade would raise the private saving rate by 0.4 percentage points.

Columns two to four of table 3-6 report equations using alternative measures of private saving adjusted for inflation and deducting capital consumption allowances. In general, they are very similar to the equation based on the unadjusted gross saving rate. The adjusted saving measure has larger residual errors, with only minor differences in the coefficients on the explanatory variables. This result was confirmed in a variant of the simple gross saving equation that included the inflation adjustment as an independent variable. Its coefficient was small and statistically insignificant. Apparently inflation illusion is a widespread phenomenon, and a large part of the inflation component of private interest income is viewed as ordinary income available to support consumption. The only significant change for net saving is the finding of a common negative trend.

The pooled regressions can also be used to investigate other issues. First, the included variables appear to do very little to explain variations in rates of saving across countries. The coefficients on the individual shift terms (not reported in the table in the interest of conserving space) are comparable to the differences observed in the mean saving rates. The range of difference in the coefficients is about 10 percent of GDP, with the United States, the United Kingdom, and Sweden at the bottom, and Japan, Germany, and Italy at the top. If the included variables fully accounted for differences in saving rates across countries, the shift terms would be zero. If the shift terms are removed from the regression, the magnitude of the coefficients on the demographic variable and income growth increases, while the other variables retain their sign and statistical significance. The average error, however, increases from 1.3 to 3.0 percent of private disposable income, and the R^2 declines from 0.92 to 0.57. This result contrasts with the cross-sectional analysis of table 3-3, in which income growth and the demographic variables accounted for a large proportion of the variation of saving rates across countries. With much smaller coefficients on income growth and demographic structure, the analysis implies that intercountry differences in saving rates are due to other factors, perhaps cultural in origin.

Second, it is possible that some common, or global, influence is missing from the specification of saving behavior, as would be the case if fluctuations in oil prices led to similar influences on saving rates in all countries. Any common factor should lead to a correlation of the error terms across countries. This hypothesis was examined by including a separate dummy variable or shift term for each of the twenty-six years in the sample. The result was that all of the coefficients were statistically insignificant, and thus the notion of common missing factors was rejected.

In general, these empirical results would suggest that lower rates of income growth are primarily responsible for reduced rates of private saving. The precise role of income growth is unclear, however. As mentioned earlier, much of modern macroeconomic theory considers consumers to be highly rational and forward-looking in planning their consumption. A long period of slower income growth, such as all these countries have experienced since 1973, should ultimately lead to a revision of expectations concerning future growth and a rise in the current saving rate for each age cohort. Although unforeseen changes in income might account for the positive correlation between contemporaneous changes in income and saving, there is no evidence in the empirical data that even lagged changes in income have a negative correlation with the saving rate. Nor was it possible to identify any other factor that might have acted as an offset to lower income growth in depressing saving rates after 1973.[23]

It is conceivable that the positive correlation between saving and income growth results from the induced shift in the distribution of aggregate income between workers (savers) and retirees (dissavers). That is the mechanism emphasized by Modigliani. However, he was able to infer that the aggregation effect would be large only by assuming that consumers are not forward-looking in anticipating future productivity growth. The change in saving within age cohorts was the focus of a recent study based on survey data from individual households collected over the past two decades in Canada, Japan, and the United States.[24] That study concluded that the decline in rates of saving is a common phenomenon for all age groups, and that the effects of changes in the age distribution on the overall saving rate have been overwhelmed by those changes within age cohorts. The finding was particularly strong for Japan, where the differences in saving rates by age groups were simply too small for shifts in the distribution of income among age cohorts to have contributed in any substantial way to the decline in household saving rates.

Both the analysis of saving rates in individual countries and the pooled regressions indicate that there is a significant negative relationship between private saving rates and the government budget deficit. Although the coefficient on the budget balance is substantially less than unity, as hypothesized by strict adherence to Barro-Ricardian equivalence, it suggests that 20–30 percent of any change in public sector saving will be offset in private saving.

The analysis provides no empirical support for arguments that attribute the decline in private saving to a surge of capital gains on existing wealth or a general aging of the population of the industrial countries.

---

23. In rejecting the version of the life cycle hypothesis in which consumers are viewed as optimizing over long horizons, the analysis is consistent with a study by Carroll and Summers (1990).

24. Bosworth, Burtless, and Sabelhaus (1991).

The results for the demographic variable are particularly surprising. Differences in the age structure of the population do have some statistical correlation with variations in saving rates across countries, but the correlation is much weaker in the time-series data. Furthermore, the largest demographic changes over the past two decades are the decline in the number of young dependents and the increased propensity to retire by the elderly, both of which should have increased the saving rate.

Investment Trends

At the beginning of the chapter the decline in private investment rates was identified as a major source of change in the domestic saving-investment balance of many countries. It was also pointed out that a decline in investment rates could be expected as a counterpart of a general trend toward lower rates of economic growth. In the long run, the growth of the stock of capital should parallel the growth in the labor force and general rates of technological advance. In the short run, countries can accelerate their rates of economic growth through increases in the ratio of capital to output; but a rise in the capital-output ratio will ultimately be reflected in a decline in the rate of return, pushing the rate of growth of the capital stock into line with that of output.

Aggregate rates of private investment were also said to have followed a pattern consistent with those basic concepts. While investment rates in Japan and Europe were substantially higher than those of the United States in the 1960s, those differences may have come about because the former were catching up to the technology and capital intensity of U.S. production. In fact, their investment rates gradually converged toward those of the United States by the late 1970s. Furthermore, there was a general decline in the share of GDP devoted to investment after 1973, which paralleled the slowdown in GDP growth.[25]

A detailed examination of the components of private investment, however, reveals a more complicated story. The representation of past trends is heavily influenced by the choice of the specific measure of investment performance. Investment rates differ substantially, depend-

---

25. The general slowing of output growth can be traced, in turn, to a slowing of technological change, as reflected in the concept of total factor productivity. See, for example, Organization for Economic Cooperation and Development (1987).

TABLE 3-7. *Private Fixed Investment, United States, Japan, and Europe, 1966–72, 1984–90*
Percent of GDP

Item	1966–72	1984–90	Change
Current prices			
Gross private investment			
United States	15.6	15.7	0.1
Japan	28.7	24.2	−4.5
Europe	19.5	17.1	−2.4
Net private investment			
United States	6.7	4.4	−2.3
Japan	15.7	7.6	−8.1
Europe	10.5	6.1	−4.4
1980 prices			
Gross private investment			
United States	17.1	17.7	0.6
Japan	26.8	26.9	0.1
Europe	20.4	18.1	−2.3
Gross business investment			
United States	11.7	12.8	1.1
Japan	19.0	21.0	2.0
Europe	12.6	13.0	0.4
Gross residential investment			
United States	5.4	5.0	−0.4
Japan	7.8	5.9	−1.9
Europe	7.8	5.0	−2.8
Net private investment			
United States	7.4	5.0	−2.4
Japan	14.7	8.5	−6.2
Europe	11.0	6.4	−4.6
Net business investment[a]			
United States	4.4	3.0	−1.4
Japan	9.0	6.6	−2.4
Europe	9.0	6.0	−3.0

SOURCES: OECD (1991b) and author's calculations as explained in the text.
a. Approximated by the change in the gross capital stock divided by GNP.

ing on whether they are measured in current or constant prices and whether they are reported in gross terms or net of the depreciation of existing capital (capital consumption allowances).

Table 3-7 illustrates the importance of the measurement issues for the United States, Japan, and an aggregate of European countries. Gross investment rates, shown at the top of the table in current prices, have fallen in Japan and Europe, but there is little indication of a slowdown in the United States. Rates of net investment, which deducts the depreciation of existing capital, show a much larger and more general pattern of decline in all three regions.

Measures of investment in constant prices, shown in the lower part of the table, tell an even more confusing story. The gross investment rate, measured in constant prices, has remained relatively stable in both the United States and Japan, whereas it has fallen in Europe. Furthermore, a disaggregation of the total into its business and residential components shows an increase in the share of GDP devoted to business investment in all three regions; evidence of a decline is limited to residential construction.[26] At the same time, rates of net investment continue to indicate a substantial falloff of business capital accumulation in all three regions, in contrast to the rates of gross investment.[27]

The divergence of these alternative investment measures can be attributed to two major developments. First, there has been a significant decline in the relative price of business capital. For Japan the price of capital goods fell by 35 percent in relation to the more general price deflator for GDP over the period 1965–1990. For the United States and Europe it is a more recent phenomenon that emerged in the 1980s, but it amounted to 20 and 10 percent, respectively, by 1990. Thus, the constant price measure of the investment share shows much less of a decline than the ratio using nominal prices.

Some of the fall in the relative price of capital reflects the growing importance of computers where technological change, which reduced the production costs of machines of equivalent computing power, has been particularly rapid. But for Japan it results from a more general improvement in the efficiency of the industries producing capital goods. In the mid-1960s Japan still used extensive trade restrictions to protect an inefficient capital goods industry. Consequently, prices of capital goods were far above international levels. By the 1980s many of Japan's

26. No effort is made to explain the variation in inventory investment. Although it is a primary source of short-run variability, inventory accumulation for many of the countries is obtained as a residual, deducting other components of final demand from an estimate of GDP based on value added. Thus, it includes any statistical discrepancy in estimating GDP.

27. The published SNA data do not provide measures of net investment in constant prices, nor do they separate capital consumption allowances for business from those for residential capital. In table 3-7 the estimate of net investment is based on the same price deflator as for gross investment. Data on net business investment in Japan and the United States were obtained from national sources. For Europe the estimate of net business investment was computed as the change in the gross capital stock, which incorporates a deduction for the scrappage of capital at the end of its estimated life, rather than annual depreciation. Thus the level of net investment is overstated for Europe.

capital goods industries were fully competitive in the global market and prices had declined to the level of other industrial countries.[28]

Second, there has been a shift in the composition of investment toward shorter-lived assets. As a result, a larger portion of each year's investment must be devoted to maintaining the existing stock, and the wedge between gross and net investment, capital consumption allowances, has increased as a share of GDP in all of these economies. The wedge has also been affected by the rise in the overall capital-output ratio within Japan and Europe, which would have increased the share of capital consumption allowances in GDP even if the average age of capital had remained unchanged. This effect is small for the United States.[29] Thus, the rates of net investment have declined more than the rates of gross investment.

Which measure should we believe? Certainly the decline in the relative cost of capital is an important phenomenon that is captured by measures of investment expressed in constant prices. The choice between gross and net rates of investment is more controversial, however. On one hand, gross investment avoids the problem of estimating depreciation, and it is appropriate for assessing the demand for current output. On the other, it is seriously flawed as a supply-side measure of capital accumulation because the composition of investment shifted toward shorter-lived assets. Investment in a unit of capital that lasts only five years is quite different from investment in capital with a useful life of ten years. The shift toward shorter-lived capital is an important phenomenon that should not be ignored solely because of difficulties in measuring depreciation. Net investment is the more meaningful supply-side concept because it measures the buildup of a stock of capital, which is more closely related to the flow of capital services into the production process.[30] Furthermore, most empirical studies of invest-

28. Measured in international prices (purchasing power parities) the share of GDP devoted to investment in Japan during the 1960s and 1970s was lower than it appeared when measured in domestic prices. Estimates of investment rates based on standard international prices are provided in the working paper by Ford and Poret (1990). By 1985, measurement in international prices had relatively little effect on measured investment rates among the major industrial countries.

29. There are substantial differences in the methods that the countries use to compute capital stocks and depreciation rates. The most significant difference is in the assumptions made about the useful lives of various kinds of capital. Japan, in particular, uses very short estimates of service lives based largely on tax laws. These differences make comparisons across countries of net investment rates highly unreliable.

30. Some recent theories of economic growth argue that gross investment is important to the growth process because it embodies new technologies. The existence of embodiments effects, however, does not reduce the importance of an accumulated stock

ment demand have had greater success modeling the process as a demand for a stock of capital with explicit allowance for replacement investment.

The data suggest that an evaluation of investment performance should distinguish between business and residential capital. The two components have behaved quite differently over time and are determined by somewhat different forces.

Business Investment

Nearly all studies of business investment behavior emphasize the importance of the positive relationship between changes in output and the level of investment, accelerator effects. Beyond that, there has been little agreement on other determinants of investment.[31] Most of the research has relied on a neoclassical model that assumes the desired stock of capital is proportionate to expected levels of output and the cost of capital. The cost of capital includes the effects of depreciation, taxes, and financing costs and is expected to have an important effect on investment through its influence on the choice among production processes of different capital intensities. Changes in the stock of capital (net investment) are then modeled as being proportionate to changes in the desired capital stock, with some allowances for adjustment lags and the formulation of expectations of future output.

At the empirical level most studies have confirmed a part of the model in that they have consistently found a strong correlation between investment and changes in output. The results for the cost of capital have been more disappointing, however, because many studies have failed to detect a statistically significant role for financing costs and taxes. In part, the empirical difficulties reflect the complexities of constructing an accurate measure of the after-tax cost of capital.[32]

Another problem is that disequilibrium factors have a strong influence on historical rates of investment. For much of the period after World War II, Europe and Japan faced a significant capital shortage as

---

of capital, and many aspects of quality improvements in capital are already reflected in the construction of the price indexes.

31. See Ford and Poret (1990) and the references they cite.

32. Some studies have attempted to circumvent the measurement problems by relating investment to changes in the ratio of the market value of capital to its replacement costs. However, these "Q" models have not been more successful at the empirical level, primarily because they are simply a transformation of the standard neoclassical theory, in which firms are assumed to equate the return from an additional unit of capital with the cost of capital, and the same measurement problems reappear in an altered context.

they lagged behind the United States in terms of the average technology incorporated in their capital stocks. That situation generated opportunities for extraordinary returns from new investment until high rates of capital accumulation gradually drove down the rate of return so that by the 1980s it was more in line with the cost of capital. Since 1980 rates of return have tended to rise, consistent with the increased real costs of borrowing in financial markets. The potential importance of disequilibrium effects suggests that there may be a role for the profit rate on existing capital as a measure of changing investment opportunities.

In view of these considerations, business investment is modeled as a function of current and past changes in output and the difference between the profit rate on existing capital and the cost of capital:

$$dK = a_1 + \sum b_i\, dQ + c_1(r_k - cc),$$

(3-11)   and

$$cc = (P_k/P_q)\,(d + rr),$$

where dK = percentage change in the capital stock, dQ = percentage change in real output, r_k = rate of return on business capital, cc = cost of capital, d = depreciation rate (0.15), and rr = real interest rate. This departs from the standard neoclassical formulation in its use of the gap between the return on physical and financial capital, rather than the change in the cost of capital.

No satisfactory measure of the marginal rate of return on business capital has yet been devised. However, the OECD does publish a measure of the before-tax gross rate of return (inclusive of depreciation) that should serve as a rough index of changes in the profitability of investment. Borrowing costs are represented by a constructed measure of the real interest rate: the long-term bond rate in each country minus a three-year average of the rate of change of capital goods prices. The cost of capital is expressed as the ratio of the price deflators for investment and output multiplied by the real rate of interest plus an allowance for depreciation of 15 percent annually. This measure excludes the effects of changes in tax policies because of the lack of adequate data. The influence of output changes is represented by a polynomial lag on the percentage change in real GDP extending over the preceding five years. By emphasizing the rate of growth of output, rather than its level, the model treats investment as an adjustment to a desired stock of capital, which is, in turn, proportionate to the level of output.

The dependent variable is the percentage change in the gross capital stock of business. In the empirical analysis the change in the capital stock performed much better in terms of goodness of fit and significance of the individual coefficients than the alternative of gross investment expressed as a percentage of GDP. The data for the United States, Canada, and the United Kingdom were adjusted to exclude investment in the petroleum industry.[33] In addition, a time trend was included to allow for potential biases in the measures of the secular trend of capital accumulation and the rate of return.

The results of estimating this model over the period 1965–90 for fourteen countries are reported in table 3-8. Despite the simplicity of the basic formulation, the model appears to capture the main features of the change in investment rates. The most consistent finding is a strong positive relationship between the rate of output growth and changes in the capital stock. This correlation supports the basic argument that the demand for capital is a stock relationship. Except for Japan, however, the output elasticity is substantially less than unity. In addition, for twelve of the fourteen countries there is a positive correlation between investment and the rate of return on existing capital, although it is often of limited statistical significance. Most countries show some evidence of a negative relationship between investment and interest rates, but the absolute magnitude of the effect is quite small.

Following the same procedures used for the saving relationships, the data were pooled and a single common regression was estimated for all of the countries. Shift terms were again included to allow for differences in the constant term across countries. The results were as follows:

$$dk = 0.12 \, dQ + 0.09 \, dQ_{-1} + 0.12 \, dQ_{-2} + 0.12 \, dQ_{-3} +$$
$$ (6.7) \qquad (4.4) \qquad\quad (6.7) \qquad\quad (7.1)$$
$$(3\text{-}12) \qquad 0.10 \, dQ_{-4} + 0.05 \, dQ_{-5} + 0.35 \, r_k - 0.09 \, rr.$$
$$\phantom{(3\text{-}12)\quad} (6.0) \qquad\quad (3.2) \qquad\quad (12.5) \quad\ (5.1)$$

$$\text{S.E.E.} = 0.6$$

The coefficients are very similar to those obtained in the regressions for individual countries. The sum of the output coefficients, 0.60, continues to indicate that the changes in the capital stock are less than

---

33. Data on energy investment were not available for Norway; because the basic relationship fit poorly, Norway was excluded from the analysis.

TABLE 3-8. *Regression Equations for Rates of Change in Business Capital Stock, by Country, 1965–90*

Country	Output growth	Rate of return on capital	Interest rate	Time trend	R^2	Standard error	Durbin- Watson
United States	0.24	0.37	−0.06	−0.07	0.94	0.3	1.2
	(1.9)	(3.5)	(1.2)	(4.6)			
Canada	0.38	0.15	−0.08	a	0.77	0.4	1.9
	(2.3)	(3.0)	(1.4)				
Japan	1.27	0.27	−0.11	a	0.99	0.3	1.5
	(8.8)	(3.7)	(2.2)				
Australia	0.32	a	a	−0.04	0.86	0.4	1.4
	(5.7)			(2.6)			
Large European countries							
France	0.54	0.11	−0.10	−0.04	0.97	0.2	1.1
	(3.5)	(1.3)	(3.2)	(1.8)			
Germany	0.65	0.24	a	a	0.91	0.4	0.8
	(4.5)	(1.9)					
United Kingdom	0.37	a	a	−0.10	0.92	0.3	1.1
	(6.8)			(13.4)			
Italy	0.23	0.27	−0.06	−0.07	0.90	0.3	1.1
	(1.7)	(2.8)	(1.8)	(3.2)			
Small European countries							
Austria	0.70	0.12	−0.31	−0.14	0.98	0.3	2.0
	(7.3)	(1.4)	(4.6)	(6.9)			
Belgium	0.47	0.13	−0.05	a	0.97	0.2	1.4
	(10.0)	(2.9)	(2.2)				
Denmark	0.42	0.11	−0.09	−0.04	0.98	0.3	2.1
	(5.6)	(1.7)	(3.2)	(4.0)			
Finland	0.45	0.14	−0.11	−0.03	0.85	0.4	0.6
	(4.3)	(1.0)	(2.1)	(1.8)			
Netherlands	0.61	0.11	−0.14	a	0.96	0.3	2.1
	(8.9)	(1.8)	(2.1)				
Sweden	0.51	0.22	−0.18	a	0.91	0.3	2.1
	(7.1)	(3.3)	(5.0)				

SOURCE: Author's calculations as explained in the text. T-statistics are in parentheses.
a. Variable excluded from regression.

fully proportionate to changes in output; the coefficient on the profit rate is large and highly significant; and although the coefficient of financing costs is statistically significant, it is small. In this case, however, the equation performs better using the real interest rate alone, rather than multiplying it by the relative price of capital goods. The reported interest rate term is an average of the preceding three years.

The positive effects of income growth are larger than the results for saving, and there is a significant interest rate effect of the expected sign. Although the coefficients on the country dummies are not reported in detail, they show less variation than those obtained from the saving equations, which implies that investment behavior is more homogeneous across countries. The coefficients on the dummy variables also indicate that, adjusted for the effects of income growth and interest rates, the United States has an unusually low rate of capital accumulation, about 3 percent per year below that of Japan and about 2 percentage points below the European average. As with saving, an alternative equation that included dummy variables for individual years indicated that the residual errors of the regression equations are generally uncorrelated across countries.

Residential Investment

Although residential construction represents only about one-fourth of private investment, it accounts for a disproportionate share of the decline in investment rates over the past twenty-five years. An international comparison of housing investment, shown in table 3-9, also reveals some surprises. First, the United States, which has been criticized for a tax system that heavily subsidizes housing investment, actually ranks near the bottom in terms of the proportion of GDP devoted to residential construction over the past several decades. Japan, whose housing is often described as grossly inadequate, has spent a larger amount of its income on housing than the United States.

The magnitude of these divergences can be reduced by focusing on the stock of housing relative to income. An estimate of the ratio of the capital stock to income can be obtained by dividing the investment shares by the rate of income growth, as was done in the introduction.[34] The implied long-run ratio of the housing stock to GDP is shown in the far right column of table 3-9. The adjustment for differences in income growth reveals a surprising degree of similarity in the implied capital-income ratios, which are all clustered around unity. On this basis, the European countries appear to allocate the largest proportion of output to housing.

---

34. This method of computing the capital-income ratio was used because of the lack of direct information on housing stocks in the individual countries. The rate of capital depreciation was assumed to be a constant 2.5 percent annually in all countries.

TABLE 3-9. *Residential Investment and Capital-Income Ratios in Fifteen OECD Countries, Selected Periods, 1965—90*

Percent of GDP, 1980 prices

Country	Investment ratio			Capital-income ratio 1965–90[a]
	Average 1965–72	Average 1984–90	Change	
United States	5.4	5.0	− 0.4	0.91
Canada	5.9	6.3	0.4	0.90
Japan	7.9	5.9	− 2.0	0.81
Australia	5.4	4.9	− 0.5	0.79
Large European countries				
France	8.6	5.7	2.9	1.21
Germany	8.6	5.6	− 3.0	1.25
Italy	10.8	5.5	− 5.3	1.23
United Kingdom	4.9	3.3	− 1.6	0.82
Small European countries				
Austria	6.3	4.8	− 1.5	0.92
Belgium	7.0	3.6	− 3.4	0.94
Denmark	8.5	4.3	− 4.2	1.17
Finland	7.5	6.0	− 1.5	1.13
Netherlands	7.7	5.5	− 2.2	1.12
Norway	4.8	4.2	− 0.6	0.75
Sweden	7.1	4.5	− 2.6	1.02

SOURCES: OECD (1991b) and author's calculations as explained in the text.

a. The implied capital-income ratio (K/Y) is obtained from the following formula: $K/Y = I/Y / (d + g)$ where d is a depreciation rate of 0.025 annually; g is the average annual growth of GDP, 1960–90; and I/Y is the average investment to GDP, 1965–90.

There are several explanations for this result. According to international comparisons of purchasing power parity, the cost of construction is very high in Japan. Thus, in international prices Japan gets very little housing for the amount of money devoted to it.[35] Furthermore, because land is relatively inexpensive in Australia, Canada, and the United States, one would expect to observe some substitution of land, which is not included in the investment data, for the structures component. Finally, although owner-occupied housing may be quite elaborate in the United States, the country's low-income housing is worse than that of most industrial countries.

35. In a 1985 comparison of purchasing power parities, the residential construction in Japan was 154 percent of the average for GDP as a whole. See Organization for Economic Cooperation and Development (1986), p. 29.

A recent study by the OECD explores in detail the factors influencing housing investment in the largest seven economies.[36] It models investment as an adjustment to a desired stock of housing and concludes that the long-run elasticities of the housing stock with respect to per capita income and population were both close to unity, but the adjustment lags were very long. In addition, it found financing costs to be important in most countries.

This analysis adopts a simpler formulation that maintains the essential features of the OECD study. The dependent variable is housing investment as a share of GDP. The long lag in the adjustment of the housing stock to changes in income is incorporated by regressing the investment rate on a ten-year average of past rates of income change (V). Financial factors are modeled as affecting the timing of the adjustment, the rate of investment directly, rather than the desired stock. Thus, the lags on interest rates are far less than those on income, and investment is related to the level, rather than the change, in interest rates. Two concepts were used to reflect financing considerations. The first was simply the level of the long-term real interest rate (r_1). The second was the differential between the short- and long-term nominal interest rates ($r_1 - r_s$). At least in countries such as the United States, where housing finance was tied to long-term financial instruments, a high short-term interest rate may result in a postponement of home purchases.

The estimated equations are shown in table 3-10. There is a positive association between housing investment and long-term rates of income growth; but the magnitude of the coefficient is highly variable across countries and generally below the long-term capital-income ratio shown in table 3-9. The estimates of the income coefficient are also quite sensitive to variation in the estimation period and the inclusion of an independent trend term. Additional experiments, based on variations in the length of the lag on income changes, confirm, however, that the process of adjustment is much slower here than for business capital. All the countries show evidence of a significant negative influence of interest rates on housing, and in many cases the effect is substantial. The interest rate differential was preferred to the level of the real interest rate in slightly less than half of the countries. The long-term decline of housing investment in these countries is largely attributed to slower rates of income growth; but the high real interest rates of the 1980s are an added factor. These results suggest that the housing

36. Egebo, Richardson, and Lienert (1990).

TABLE 3-10. *Regression Equations for Residential Investment, 1970–90*

Country	Income growth	Interest rates		R^2	Standard error	Durbin-Watson
		Level	Differential			
United States	0.70	− 0.10	− 0.46	0.86	0.3	1.5
	(5.4)	(4.6)	(7.4)			
Canada	0.41	− 0.07	− 0.16	0.66	0.3	1.4
	(1.6)	(3.2)	(3.2)			
Japan	0.42	− 0.09	a	0.82	0.6	0.9
	(7.0)	(2.7)				
Australia	0.09	a	− 0.29	0.71	0.3	1.2
	(1.8)		(5.7)			
Large European countries						
France	0.93	− 0.07	a	0.94	0.4	0.7
	(12.4)	(2.1)				
Germany	0.53	− 0.18	a	0.87	0.4	1.0
	(4.7)	(4.3)				
Italy	1.42	a	− 0.24	0.93	0.5	1.6
	(11.6)		(3.7)			
United Kingdom	0.62	a	− 0.14	0.59	0.4	0.9
	(4.0)		(3.0)			
Small European countries						
Austria	0.23	− 0.05	a	0.88	0.2	1.6
	(5.6)	(2.6)				
Belgium	0.62	− 0.15	a	0.82	0.7	1.3
	(3.6)	(3.4)				
Denmark	2.08	a	− 0.32	0.92	0.7	1.6
	(12.0)		(2.3)			
Finland	0.72	− 0.10	a	0.71	0.5	0.6
	(3.7)	(3.2)				
Netherlands	0.44	− 0.23[b]	a	0.84	0.4	1.7
	(7.3)	(3.2)				
Norway	0.81	− 0.08[b]	a	0.71	0.3	1.4
	(6.6)	(2.2)				
Sweden	0.28	− 0.03	a	0.43	0.3	0.8
	(1.8)	(1.6)				

SOURCE: Author's calculations as explained in the text. T-statistics are in parentheses.
a. Variable not in regression.
b. Change in the interest rate.

market plays a role in the balancing of domestic saving and investment that is disproportionate to its size because it is more sensitive than business investment to interest rate changes.

The regression based on pooled data yielded few new results. The coefficient on long-run income growth averages 0.58, and the level of interest rates and the interest rate differential are of about equal statistical significance:

$$(3\text{-}13) \qquad I/GDP = 0.58\,V - 0.05\,rr_{-1} - 0.10\,diff_{-1}$$
$$\qquad\qquad\quad (13.7) \qquad (4.5) \qquad\quad (3.6) \qquad \text{S.E.E.} = 0.75.$$

The coefficients on the country dummies are not shown, but they implied that, adjusted for income growth and interest rates, the investment rate was lowest in the United Kingdom and the United States and highest in continental Europe.

The Private Saving-Investment Balance

The main result that emerges from the preceding sections is that private rates of saving and investment are linked over the long term, moving up and down together in response to variations in the growth of the overall economy. Whereas the correlation between investment and income growth is expected because of strong theoretical considerations, the extent of the correlation between saving rates and income growth is more of a surprise.

Although economic growth plays an influential role in all countries, the private saving-investment balance has varied sharply over time and among countries as slower rates of economic growth have had a more pronounced depressive influence on investment than saving. In fact, the industrial countries as a whole had a surplus of private saving in relation to private investment needs during the 1980s. As figure 3-2 shows, the private SI balance in Japan and Europe shifted from a deficit in the 1960s to substantial surpluses by the mid-1980s. In Japan the surplus of private saving over private investment exceeded 4 percent of NDP in 1981–85, compared with an average deficit of only 0.7 percent in the 1965–72 period. For Europe, the shift was from a small deficit in the 1965–72 period to a surplus in excess of 4 percent of NDP in the mid-1980s. The Japanese surplus vanished at the end of the 1980s under the impetus of a continued gradual decline in the saving rate and a surge of domestic investment, but the investment boom came to an end in

FIGURE 3-2. *Private Saving-Investment Balance and the Governmental Budget Balance, Three Industrial Economies, 1965–90*

Percent of net domestic product

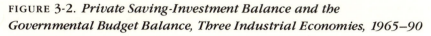

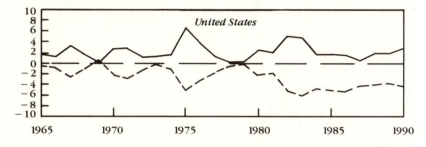

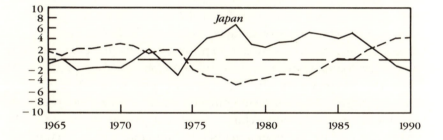

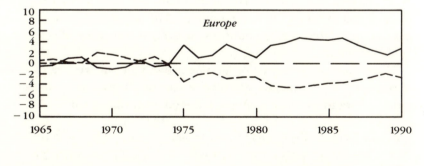

——————— Private SI balance   – – – –   Government budget balance

SOURCE: OECD (1991b).

the early 1990s. A similar but less dramatic evolution of the balance occurred in Europe.

The United States is a significant exception in that there is no evident trend in the SI balance; it was 1.8 percent of NDP in the 1965–72 period and averaged 2.4 percent in the 1980s. Private rates of saving and investment have gradually drifted down in parallel; and the drop in the investment rate up to the mid-1980s was less than for other countries, although from a much lower initial level. In the latter part of the 1980s the net investment rate fell further in the United States, while it was turning around and moving back up in Japan and Europe. According to the earlier statistical analysis, the divergent behavior of investment in the United States, Europe, and Japan in the late 1980s was primarily due to differences in real interest rates, which were very high in the United States and low in the other areas.

An additional test was done to examine the correlation between the residuals of the saving equation and the two investment equations. A significant correlation would suggest a missing common influence. All three residuals were rescaled to express them as a percentage of NDP and were found to be uncorrelated with one another in all of the countries. Furthermore, the addition of the private investment rate to the previously estimated saving rate equations, or vice versa, produced no significant coefficients. Thus, whatever is missing from the explanation for each of the components does not appear to be common to the others. The standard deviations of the errors in predicting the private saving-investment balance for each country generally ranged from 0.5 to 1.5 percent of NDP for those thirteen countries with regression estimates for all three components. The fact that SI residuals were also uncorrelated across countries suggests the absence of a common global influence.

The dominant influence of income growth and interest rates as determinants of the private SI balance can be illustrated by using the pooled data to estimate a simple reduced-form relationship.

$$(S - I)/GDP = -0.51\,dQ_{-1} - 0.27\,dQ_{-2} - 0.29\,dQ_{-3} - 0.07\,dQ_{-4}.$$

$$(3\text{-}14) \qquad \begin{array}{cccc} (7.3) & (3.9) & (4.2) & (1.2) \end{array}$$

$$+\,0.21\,\text{arr}$$

$$(3.5) \qquad\qquad\qquad\qquad \text{S.E.E.} = 2.6$$

The sum of the coefficients on income growth implies that a permanent reduction in the growth rate will raise the private saving-investment balance by 1.14 percent of GDP, and a 1 percent change in the real interest rate would change the balance by 0.2 percent of GDP.

Taxes and Inflation

The role of taxes is an important factor that has been largely ignored in prior sections. It was not possible to obtain data of the type required to construct meaningful time-series measures of either the effective tax for private saving or private investment. That need not be a major problem if taxes are unimportant as determinants of saving or investment or if effective tax rates have not changed substantially within individual countries. However, a study by Tamin Bayoumi and Joseph Gagnon suggests that the interaction of the tax system with inflation has resulted in large variation in effective tax rates and that taxes help explain international differences in current account balances.[37] The authors point out that, since the tax systems of most countries fail to index capital income and interest expenses for inflation, a high rate of inflation should increase the tax wedge between the interest payments made by companies and the capital income received by households.

In such a world, an acceleration of inflation expands incentives to invest in physical capital by raising the real value of interest deductions to business firms. That is to say, a portion of the nominal interest payment is a repayment of principal on the real value of the loan, but the whole payment is deductible for tax purposes. Meanwhile, the attractiveness of saving declines, unless nominal interest rates rise more than proportionately to inflation, as would be required to keep the after-tax return unchanged. As a result, an increased rate of inflation should raise domestic investment in relation to saving and thus create a current account deficit. Capital should flow from countries with a low inflation rate to those with a high inflation rate. In this argument changes in the rate of inflation are more important than changes in tax rates because of the way inflation interacts with the tax system.

Bayoumi and Gagnon argue that time-series data are inappropriate for testing the hypothesis because international capital transactions were subject to controls before the 1980s. Instead, they used data from a set of industrial countries comparable to that used in this study to construct a cross-sectional analysis. They averaged the data for various subperiods over the interval 1973 to 1990. They then attempted to

37. Bayoumi and Gagnon (1992).

TABLE 3-11. *Regression Estimates for Inflation and the Current Account, Fifteen Industrial Countries, Selected Periods, 1976–90*

Period	Inflation	Fiscal stance	Unemployment	R^2
Current account				
1976–80	−0.02	−0.31	−0.06	0.20
	(0.10)	(1.40)	(0.08)	
1981–85	−0.23	0.24	0.11	0.27
	(0.87)	(1.30)	(0.15)	
1986–90	−1.24	0.04	0.70	0.76
	(5.40)	(0.32)	(1.50)	
Private saving-				
investment balance				
1976–80	0.26	n.a.	−2.06	0.21
	(0.73)		(1.59)	
1981–85	0.21	n.a.	1.55	0.16
	(.53)		(1.50)	
1986–90	−1.44	n.a.	2.03	0.50
	(2.51)		(1.88)	

SOURCE: Author's calculations as explained in the text. All data represent averages over a five-year period. T-statistics are in parentheses.
n.a. Not applicable.

determine if differences in current account balances correlate with differences in rates of inflation. Their model is of the following form:

$$(3\text{-}11) \quad (SUR/GDP) = b_0 + b_1\pi + b_2(NL_g/GDP) + b_3U,$$

where SUR/GDP = the ratio of the current account to GDP, π = inflation rate, NL_g = ratio of the government budget balance to GDP, and U = the deviation of the unemployment rate from its historical average. The fiscal variable is included to reflect the influence of government fiscal policies, and the unemployment rate to adjust for differences in capacity utilization. Bayoumi and Gagnon found that the extent of any correlation between the current account and inflation varied among the subperiods, but the correlation was particularly close in the late 1980s when most capital controls had been removed.

It is possible to duplicate the Bayoumi-Gagnon tests with the current data set. The results of estimating equation 3-11 for three subperiods (1976–80, 1981–85, and 1986–90) are shown in table 3-11. The inflation variable has a negative coefficient in all three subperiods and it is highly significant in one. The basic mechanism that Bayoumi and Gagnon describe, however, really applies to the private SI balance; and one would expect the government fiscal balance to be a necessary adjustment to convert to an explanation of the current account. The insignificant role of the budget balance is puzzling, therefore, except to those who believe in Ricardo-Barro equivalence between public and private saving.

A more direct test of the hypothesis is shown in the bottom part of the table, where the current account is replaced with the average of the private SI balance. In this case the inflation variable is of the wrong sign and statistically insignificant in two of the subperiods. Although differences in inflation work less well to explain variations in the SI balance, inflation is still statistically significant in 1986–90. Also, the deterioration in performance can be attributed largely to Italy, whose large private sector saving surplus is offset by a large government budget deficit. The exclusion of Italy greatly improves the fit for 1986–90, but this has little effect on the other periods.[38]

The existence of external capital controls is not a plausible explanation for the failure of the equations in the periods prior to 1986. Although external capital controls will alter the behavioral relationships determining the current account, they should not affect the relationships for private saving and investment. Instead, if an acceleration of inflation opened up a wedge between planned investment and planned saving, it would be closed by a rise in the real rate of interest. In other words, within a closed economy the interaction between taxes and inflation should lead to a positive association between the real interest rate and inflation. The inclusion of the real rate of interest, however, had no significant effect on the regressions reported in table 3-11. In general, the analysis of the private SI balance suggests that the Bayoumi and Gagnon results for the current account, although striking, may reflect a spurious correlation.

Net Saving of the Public Sector

If the current account depended only on the shift in the private saving-investment balance, most industrial countries should have had current account surpluses after 1973, as they sought to sustain domestic

---

38. One potential problem with the private SI balance as opposed to the current account is the ambiguity in dividing national saving between the public and private sectors in the presence of inflation. A reestimation of the model using the inflation-adjusted measure of private saving yielded similar results, however.

production by exporting their excess saving. Furthermore, the variation in the private SI balance has been large, despite the common correlation with income growth. The smallest standard deviation of the annual SI balance over the 1965–90 period was 1.7 percent of NDP for the United States, with other countries falling within the range of 2.5 to 4.0 percent of NDP. Yet, variations in the private SI balance have had surprisingly little implication for the current account. The correlation between the two, measured as a share of NDP, is statistically significant at the .05 level for only seven of the fifteen countries in the sample, and two of those were Norway and the United Kingdom, which had already established a strong link between energy exports and private saving.

Variations in the private SI balance are not more strongly reflected in the current account because of offsetting changes in the public sector balance. A tendency toward increased government budget deficits after 1973 is evident in figure 3-2, which shows the budget deficit as a share of NDP for the United States, Japan, and the European aggregate. But the extent of the offset goes beyond a correlation of common trends. The correlation between the government budget balance and the private SI balance is negative for all fifteen countries, even after allowing for a common trend; and it is statistically significant in thirteen. The exceptions are Australia and Norway. An illustrative equation using the pooled data for thirteen countries is shown at the top of table 3-12.[39] Fully 80 percent of any change in the government budget deficit appears to be reflected in an offsetting change in the private SI balance.

The result is simply another way of stating the familiar finding of Martin Feldstein and Charles Horioka that the domestic components of the identity linking the saving-investment balance to the current account are correlated with one another.[40] The authors interpreted the correlation between national saving (including the public sector balance) and domestic investment as evidence of restrictions on international flows of financial capital, arguing that in a world of fully mobile capital, domestic rates of saving and investment should be independent of one another. The correlation reported here differs from the Feldstein-Horioka formulation only in the rearrangement of the domestic components of the identity. The correlation first reported by Feldstein and Horioka has been reexamined numerous times since their article was

---

39. Finland and Norway were eliminated from the data set because of the lack of data on a cyclically adjusted measure of the budget deficit, a measure that is used at a later stage in the analysis.

40. Feldstein and Horioka (1980).

TABLE 3-12. *Pooled Regression Equations for Public and Private Saving Balances, Thirteen Countries, 1966–90*[a]

(1) $(S\text{-}I)/NDP = -0.81\ NL_g/NDP$
    (21.0)
                    $SEE = 1.86$

(2) $(S\text{-}I)/NDP = -0.82\ \tilde{N}\tilde{L}_g/NDP$
    (15.03)
                    $SEE = 2.19$

(3) $\tilde{N}\tilde{L}_g/NDP = 0.16\ SUR/NDP + 0.18\ SUR(-1) - 0.69\ UNR(-1) + 0.46\ UNR(-2)$
    (1.8) (2.0) (4.5) (3.0)
                                                            $SEE = 2.08$

(4) $\tilde{N}\tilde{L}_g/NDP = 0.19\ dQ(-1) + 0.15\ dQ(-2) + 0.16\ dQ(-3) + 0.17\ dQ(-4)$
    (3.5) (2.9) (3.2) (3.5)
                                                            $SEE = 2.02$

(5) $(S-I)/NDP = 0.83\ \hat{S}_p - 0.90\ \hat{I}_p - 0.28\ NL_g/NDP$
    (16.2) (15.0) (5.8)
                                                    $SEE = 1.24$

(6) $(S-I)/NDP = 0.90\ \hat{S}_p - 1.07\ \hat{I}_p - 0.15\ \tilde{N}\tilde{L}_g/NDP$
    (16.6) (19.9) (2.9)
                                                    $SEE = 1.30$

SOURCE: Author's calculations as explained in the text. T-statistics are in parentheses.

a. $(S\text{-}I)/NDP$ is the private saving-investment balance as a percent of NDP, NL_g/NDP is the government budget balance as a percent of NDP, $\tilde{N}\tilde{L}_g/NDP$ is the cyclically adjusted budget balance as a percent of NDP, SUR/NDP is the current account as a percent of NDP, dQ is the percentage change in real output, UNR is the unemployment rate (percent), $\hat{S}_p$ is the predicted values of private saving rate, and $\hat{I}_p$ is the predicted values of private investment rate.

first published. It is robust over a wide range of different countries, and the evidence of any weakening of the correlation during the 1980s, when capital markets were alleged to have become more open, is decidedly mixed.[41]

Although restrictions on international financial transactions may explain the situation in part, it is also important to note that the identity linking the current account to the domestic SI balance refers to the markets for real goods and services, not financial capital. Thus, the correlation between the domestic components could reflect barriers to international financial transactions or rigidities in the adjustment of trade flows, less than perfect substitution between domestic and foreign goods.[42] Furthermore, a negative correlation between the public and private SI balances is expected from the earlier finding that some inverse correlation exists between private saving and government budget

41. Frankel (1986) and Tesar (1988).
42. See Frankel (1986).

deficits. However, the coefficient is far above the value obtained from the private saving regressions.

The added correlation appears to result from several influences. First, changes in the budget balance will influence the private SI balance through changes in interest rates and income, channels that are both allowed for in the specification of the individual saving and investment equations but excluded from the aggregate equation of table 3-12.

In addition, the correlation could result from the behavior of the public sector, such as an endogenous response of the public budget to the business cycle. Periods of recession, when investment demand is weak in relation to saving, are also associated with increases in the budget deficit through the loss of revenues and increases in some expenditure programs, such as unemployment insurance. These so-called automatic stabilizers induce a countercyclical pattern to the budget balance.

When the cyclical component of the budget balance is eliminated, however, its correlation with the private SI balance is little affected. Using data from the OECD it is possible to estimate the sensitivity of the tax and expenditure system to changes in economic activity, and to adjust the reported budget balances to correspond to a constant rate of capacity utilization.[43] In the pooled regressions equation (see equation 2 in table 3-12, the coefficient on the structural budget balance is essentially unchanged and there is a trivial increase in the standard error of the regression. For individual countries, the correlation becomes statistically insignificant at the 0.05 level for four (Belgium, Germany, the United Kingdom, and the United States) of the thirteen countries for which data were available. For the others, however, the relationship reflects something more than just the operation of automatic stabilizers.

It has also been argued that government policies aimed at targeting either the exchange rate or the trade balance could be responsible for the Feldstein and Horioka finding.[44] Because governments are opposed to large current account imbalances, they adjust their policies so as to prevent changes in the private SI balance from passing through into changes in the current account. Moreover, because, at least on an ex ante basis, a surplus of saving over investment is associated with weak aggregate demand, the correlation may also reflect the efforts of gov-

---

43. Estimates of the marginal sensitivity of the deficit to variations in GDP were taken from Muller and Price (1984). The deficits were adjusted to correspond to the measure of capacity GDP reported in OECD (1991c).

44. Examples are provided by Tobin (1983) and Westphal (1983).

ernments to stabilize domestic demand and employment. This issue was examined by estimating a reaction function for government in which annual changes in the structural budget balance were related to the current and preceding year's current account balance, and the unemployment rate in the preceding two years. The expectation was that if either of these two indicators are important determinants of fiscal policy, their coefficients should be negative. As shown by equation 3 in the table 3-12, the results were of limited value, as the current account had a positive and insignificant effect on discretionary fiscal policy. There is an obvious bias in relating the budget balance to the concurrent change in the current account, but the results were unaffected by limiting the current account to lagged values. There is some evidence, however, that discretionary policy does respond to both the level and change in the domestic unemployment rate.

Alternatively, many of the fiscal difficulties faced by the OECD countries after 1973 may be traced to their inertia in adjusting their expectations and their expenditure programs to a lower rate of economic growth and thus revenue growth.[45] As a result, the observed correlation between net saving of the public and private sector could result from the influence of a third factor, unanticipated changes in income growth. Equation 4 of table 3-12 illustrates this process by relating the cyclically adjusted budget balance to the rate of change of real GDP in preceding years, including country-specific dummy variables. The coefficients on prior rates of income growth are statistically significant for four years, and the cumulative sum implies that following a 1 percentage point reduction in real growth the deficit would rise to 0.67 percent of NDP before leveling out.[46] Even if this endogenous element of the budget balance is excluded, however, there is still a significant correlation between the residual changes and the private SI balance. If the residuals of equation 4 in table 3-12 are used in place of the structural budget deficit in equation 2, the coefficient is 0.67 with a t-statistic of 9.7. Something other than a common influence of income growth appears to be responsible for the observed correlation.

The correlation between the private and public SI balances can be sharply reduced by incorporating the factors that are included in the

45. See, for example, Roubini and Sachs (1989).
46. In concept, the equation should be formulated in a way that constrains the long-run effect on the budget deficit of a permanent change in the growth rate to be zero. An alternative formulation that incorporated such a constraint after ten years had no significant effect on the regression, however. There is simply too little variation in the data to determine whether the constraint applies.

individual structural equations for private saving and investment. For example, if the predicted values from the regression equations for private saving and investment, presented in prior sections, are included in a regression that relates the private SI balance to the budget balance, as shown in equation 5 of table 3-12, the coefficient on the budget balance drops to 0.28. The further step of excluding the cyclical component of the budget reduces the coefficient to 0.15 (see equation 6 of table 3-12).

These tests support the argument of Feldstein and Horioka that individual countries are not so completely integrated into a global economy as to make national saving and investment independent of one another. Changes in the government budget balance result in offsetting changes in the private SI balance rather than spilling over fully into the current account. Furthermore, the equations that incorporate income growth and interest rates as determinants of private saving and investment capture the basic mechanism relating the domestic elements of the saving-investment identity to one another. The conclusion of less than full integration seems less strong for the United States, the United Kingdom, and Germany, where the correlation between the private SI balance and the cyclically adjusted measure of the public sector budget balance was very low.

Summary

The foregoing analysis suggests that the general decline in rates of private saving and investment within the industrial countries can be largely traced to a general slowing of income growth. That slowdown in turn reflects a reduced rate of technological innovation, as evidenced by a slower growth of total factor productivity after 1973. On the investment side, the effects of income growth are strong and fully expected, in keeping with standard theoretical models. However, the positive association between saving and income growth is more inconsistent with conventional models of consumer behavior.

The effort to relate private saving behavior to other factors that have been suggested in the literature yielded less conclusive results. There was no consistent evidence of a positive effect of interest rates, despite the exceptionally wide variation in real rates of interest that occurred over the 1980s. In fact, the coefficient was significantly negative in the pooled regressions. There was also no empirical support for the claim that capital gains are responsible for the decline of private saving during the 1980s; there was no correlation of private saving with changes in stock market prices for any of the countries in the sample. Capital gains on real estate may have been important, but if that were true Japan should have had a much larger decline in saving, given the extraordinary runup of land prices there.

Furthermore, the analysis tended to discount the claim that a general aging of the population in the industrial countries reduced private saving in the past or that it will do so in the future. One reason is that past demographic changes should have increased rather than reduced the private saving rate over the past two decades; that effect was only weakly evident in the time-series data. In addition, it appears from survey data that differences in saving rates among age groups are simply too small for demographic changes to have a noticeable impact.

For private investment, it appears that a simple accelerator model that emphasizes the rate of output growth cam provide an explanation for changes in the share of GDP devoted to investment, but it also indicates statistically significant effects of variations in real interest rates. One surprising result was that much of the decline in overall rates of private investment was concentrated in the residential investment sector.

The determinants of private saving and investment alone suggest that nearly all of the industrial countries should have had significant current account deficits after the slowing of economic growth in the mid-1970s. The fact that such deficits did not occur can be traced to the changed behavior of governments, which began to dissave at a far larger rate than in the past. Increases in the government budget deficit absorbed the excess of the private saving-investment balance.

This analysis does not fully explain why the change in budget policy occurred. It does not appear to be due to a direct effort of the government to balance the current account; but neither is it clear whether the change was coincidental with, or a response to, the private saving-investment surplus. The results are at least consistent with the argument that barriers to international mobility of resources are still sufficiently strong in most countries to force a balancing of domestic saving and investment through changes in interest rates and income.

Note, too, that efforts to link the current account to a specific component of the domestic SI balance—as was done in the United States in references to the twin deficits of the budget and the trade balance—are in general misleading. There have been important shifts in both the private and public balances, and no one alone provides a reliable indicator of the current account.

FIGURE 3A-1. *Saving and Investment Rates, Twelve Countries, 1965–90*

Percent of net domestic product

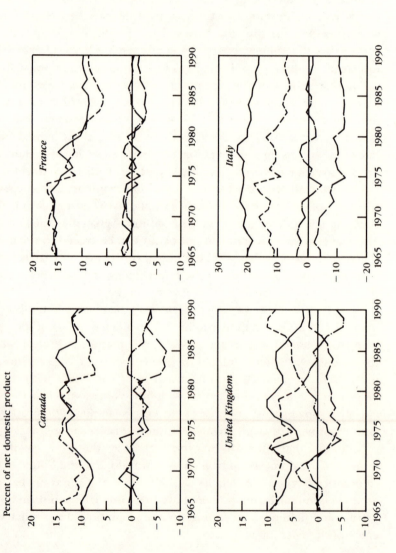

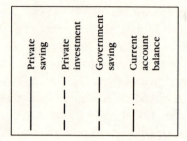

FIGURE 3A-1. (cont'd)

Percent of net domestic product

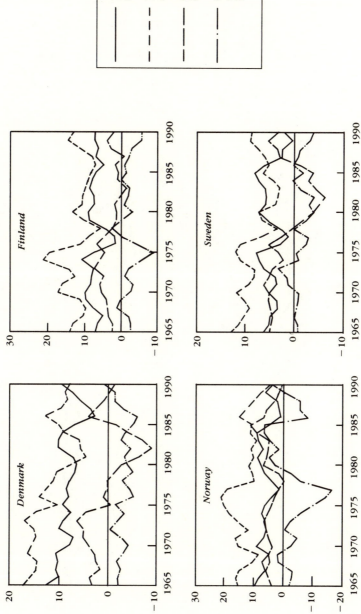

Private
saving

Private
investment

Government
saving

Current
account
balance

FIGURE 3A-1. (cont'd)

Percent of net domestic product

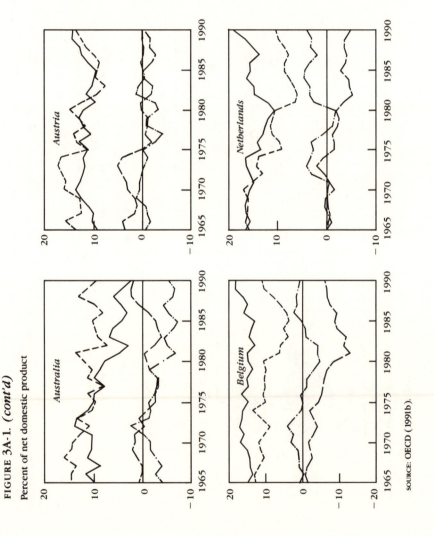

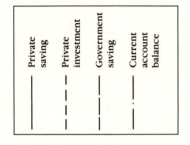

Private
saving

Private
investment

Government
saving

Current
account
balance

SOURCE: OECD (1991b).

4

Exchange Rate Mechanics: Some Empirical Tests

The exchange rate and the mechanism that determines it tie national economies together in a global system. The importance of the exchange rate in defining the competitiveness of a nation's products in international markets was vividly illustrated by the runup of the dollar in the mid-1980s and its subsequent collapse: faced with nearly a 50 percent rise in their prices, American exporters lost a substantial share of their global market. It also plays a critical role, as discussed in chapters 1 and 2, in the mechanism tying the current account to the domestic saving-investment balance. All the same, little agreement has yet been reached on the determinants of the exchange rate.

The debate over the determinants of exchange rates rests on the question of the extent of integration of financial markets internationally. In a world of open capital markets with a free flow of funds across national boundaries, investors should allocate their investment portfolios between foreign and domestic assets until the two expected rates of return are equal. And, as reported in chapter 1, there is substantial evidence that arbitrage between markets has by and large eliminated the interest rate differential for financial instruments, negotiated in a common currency, among international financial markets. Investments denominated in a foreign currency raise a different set of issues. The advantage of investing in a foreign market with a higher rate of return can be quickly wiped out by a relatively minor but unforeseen change in the exchange rate.[1]

---

1. If a large proportion of the investor's consumption is devoted to traded goods whose prices are set in a global market, a portion of the financial loss of unforeseen

Thus, even if investors did act to equalize expected rates of return on alternative assets, national interest rates would differ because of expected changes in the exchange rate. In fact, differences in national interest rates are widely thought to indicate investors' expectations of future exchange rate changes.

Many economists would assert that we cannot forecast future exchange rate movements beyond accounting for this expected component, as revealed in interest rate differentials; and, if we rule out inside information, we should not expect to be able to. In an efficient market all current information should be fully reflected in current prices of alternative financial assets. In highly developed domestic financial markets, for example, forecasts of even the direction of change in future bond prices is a fifty-fifty proposition. It should not be possible to exploit profitably the forecast of tomorrow's exchange rate any more than investors would be able to consistently profit from their forecasts of future movements in the domestic bond market.

It is quite different, however, to argue that we cannot explain exchange rate movements, even after they have occurred, or that we cannot provide useful predictions of the exchange rate response to a proposed change in economic policy. Yet, many economists who have evaluated the empirical performance of the various exchange rate theories have reached that conclusion.[2] Despite the lack of empirical support, strongly stated propositions about the determinants of exchange rates continue to be central features of the analytical models that are used to advance recommendations on economic policy.

The purpose of this chapter is to provide an empirical assessment of the leading hypotheses that have been advanced to explain exchange rate movements. It differs from previous studies in two respects. First, most of the empirical evaluations have focused on the relationship between the U.S. dollar and other major currencies. The problem is, the dollar's price may be influenced by factors that are different from those that determine other bilateral exchange rates because of its role as an international medium of exchange. Thus, evidence on the performance of the models relative to dollar-based bilateral rates may not apply to the more general case. This study extends some of the previous

---

exchange rate changes is offset by a compensatory change in the price of consumption. This provides a rationale for holding an internationally diversified portfolio.

2. Meese and Rogoff (1983, 1988).

research by testing identical specifications of the models with exchange rate data for 16 countries.[3]

Second, most of the prior empirical research has focused on bilateral exchange rates, such as the relative price of the dollar against the Japanese yen, or the dollar against the German mark. This emphasis on individual bilateral rates may be an unduly harsh test of the ability of a model to explain relative prices. It requires full information not only on economic events in each of the two countries in question, but also on economic conditions in all other economies that affect the two in a differential fashion. The present analysis examines the behavior of composite trade-weighted exchange rates. By aggregating the exchange rates of the competitor countries, we can eliminate many of the covariances and focus more directly on the difference between domestic and overall foreign economic conditions in attempting to account for a change in the relative value of a country's currency. Changes in the exchange rate in relation to an average of competitor countries also seem far more relevant for explaining trade flows, which are the subject of chapter 5.

The next section highlights the differences in the basic assumptions that motivate the principal models of exchange rate behavior and derives formulations that can be tested empirically. The remainder of the chapter reports results of the empirical analysis, which is based largely on quarterly data extending over the 1973–90 period. Quarterly data are used here instead of annual data because of their availability and also because of their sensitivity and faster response to events in financial markets.

Alternative Theories of Exchange Rate Determination

The numerous models of exchange rate determination proposed in the economic literature differ primarily in their treatment of the degree of integration of national economies into a global system.[4] The first point of contention—as is seen in the debate surrounding purchasing power parity—is the extent of integration of goods markets, the question being, how freely interchangeable are domestic and foreign-pro-

---

3. The list of countries included in the empirical analysis differs from that of the prior chapter because of differences in the availability of data.

4. The material in this section draws heavily on overview papers by Dornbusch (1980a) and Frankel (1983).

duced goods? The second point concerns the extent of integration of financial markets and has arisen in the debate over the concept of uncovered interest rate parity.

Purchasing power parity (PPP), as discussed in chapter 2, implies that domestic and foreign goods are perfect substitutes. This notion has great bearing on the exchange rate: if domestic and foreign-produced goods are perfect substitutes—viewed as identical products by consumers—their prices will be equal when measured in a common currency. Thus, under the assumption of PPP, the nominal exchange rate is simply the ratio of the domestic level (P) to the level of foreign prices (P^*), or

$$(4\text{-}1) \qquad\qquad e = P/P^*.$$

As explained in chapter 2, there are several obvious exceptions to PPP in its most extreme form, but many theories of exchange rate determination still incorporate it as a basic long-run assumption.

Uncovered interest rate parity implies that domestic and foreign bonds are perfect substitutes.[5] If UIP is assumed to hold, domestic and foreign bonds of equivalent risk and maturity must earn equal rates of return after adjusting for any expected change in the exchange rate. If so, the relationship can be reversed to obtain estimates of expected exchange rate changes. The expected change in the exchange rate over a future period, T, is equal to the interest differential on domestic and foreign bonds measured over the same horizon:

$$(4\text{-}2) \qquad \Delta e^e_T = e - E(e_T) = i_T - i^*_T, \text{ or}$$
$$e = E(e_T) + i_T - i^*_T.$$

Like PPP, this simple version of UIP has some drawbacks (see chapter 2), but the link between international interest rate differentials and expected exchange rate changes is critical to many exchange rate models and the standard view of the adjustment mechanism, as reflected in the Mundell-Fleming model. A rise in the domestic interest rate is interpreted as a signal of a domestic capital shortage, and it leads

---

5. It is useful to make a clear distinction, as provided by Frankel (1983), between capital mobility and substitutability. Capital mobility refers only to the institutional changes that permit investors to freely move funds between national capital markets and thus allow them to adjust their portfolios to desired levels. Perfect substitutes institute a much stronger statement about investors' views of the distinction between domestic and foreign bonds.

to an inflow of capital, increased demand for the domestic currency, and an appreciation of the exchange rate above its long-run value. These reactions continue until investors feel confident that the risk of returning to a more normal exchange rate in the future (an exchange rate loss) counterbalances the gains from the higher interest rate. The currency appreciation, in turn, implies a rise in the price of domestic versus foreign-produced goods, and a subsequent worsening of the trade balances. If the response to interest rate differentials is not an important part of the process determining the exchange rate, much of the basic explanation of the international adjustment mechanism will have to be re-thought.

The implications for exchange rate behavior of assumptions about the extent of substitution between domestic and foreign goods and between domestic and foreign bonds are explored more fully in the following sections. Those models that incorporate PPP as either a short-run or equilibrium condition are generally treated as monetary models because real factors play no role in the determination of the equilibrium exchange rate. Those that reject PPP as an equilibrium condition are referred to as real models. Most alternatives to UIP treat exchange rates from the perspective of portfolio-balance models.

Monetary Models

For many years theoretical explanations of exchange rate determination rested on the notion that the exchange rate is determined primarily by monetary forces and that real factors play only an indirect role, through their influence on the relative demands for money. That is, monetary models assume that equilibrium exchange rates are determined by purchasing power parity. It is possible to distinguish several variants of the monetary model, depending on whether they assume that PPP holds in the short run, completely flexible prices, or only in the long run, sticky prices. These variants also differ in whether they impose UIP in addition to the PPP assumption.

THE FLEXIBLE-PRICE MODEL.[6] For the sake of simplicity, assume a two-country world in which all foreign variables are denoted with an asterisk. If goods must sell at the same price in all markets (PPP), the nominal exchange rate is simply the ratio of two average price levels, or, in logarithmic form,

---

6. Frenkel (1976) and Bilson (1978).

(4-3) $$e = p - p^*.$$

Thus the only task is to explain the evolution of the domestic and foreign price levels. If prices are fully flexible and allow economies to operate continuously at full employment, changes in the price level are fully determined by monetary factors. Assume that each country's money supply (m) is set exogenously and that the two money demand functions are expressed in terms of the price level (p), real income (y), and interest rates (i). Again in logarithms,

(4-4a) $$m_d = p + \beta_1 y - \beta_2 i$$
(4-4b) $$m_d^* = p^* + \beta_1 y^* - \beta_2 i^*.\,[7]$$

Substituting 4-4a and 4-4b into equation 4-3 yields an explanation of the exchange rate as solely a function of monetary developments:

(4-5) $$e = (m - m^*) - \beta_1(y - y^*) + \beta_2(i - i^*).$$

The underlying logic of the relationship is that an increase in the domestic money supply will cause a currency depreciation (a rise in e) because, with fixed levels of income and interest rates, the increase can be absorbed only through a rise in the price level, and, thus, a depreciation of the exchange rate to maintain PPP. Similarly, an increase in income will be associated with a higher demand for money, which requires a reduction in the price level and currency appreciation. The sign of the interest rate effect may seem more surprising, but a higher interest rate will lead to a reduced demand for money balances, and it will only be possible to absorb the excess by a price increase and a currency depreciation. As the interest rate feature makes clear, equation 4-5 should be interpreted as an equilibrium condition between the exchange rate and the other variables rather than a direct causal relationship. An increase in the interest rate leads to a depreciation of the currency only if there is no change in real income or in the money supply. The usefulness of the monetary model as an empirical framework also depends on the assumption that the two money demand functions are stable and that the possible inconsistencies in the construction of national price levels, mentioned in chapter 2, are not severe.

---

7. The assumption that the coefficients of the money demand functions are identical in the two regions is adopted for the sake of simplicity and is not critical to the basic conclusions.

An alternative version of the flexible-price model can be derived by further assuming perfect substitutability between domestic and foreign bonds (UIP), as well as between domestic and foreign goods. Ignoring time subscripts, equation 4-2 can be restated as

$$(4\text{-}6) \qquad\qquad i - i^* = \Delta e^e.$$

If PPP is expected to hold at all points in time, the expected rate of exchange depreciation should equal the expected inflation differential,

$$(4\text{-}7) \qquad \Delta e^e = (\Delta p)^e - (\Delta p^*)^e = (\pi - \pi^*).$$

Thus, one can replace the interest rate differential of equation 4-5 with the expected inflation differential to obtain

$$(4\text{-}8) \qquad e = (m - m^*) - b_1(y - y^*) + b_2(\pi - \pi^*).$$

Equations 4-5 and 4-8 demonstrate the influence of the two basic assumptions of PPP and UIP. Under conditions of PPP all goods are sold in a single global market, and domestic demand conditions have no influence on the output of domestic firms. It is a global economy in which any required reallocation of domestic demand between domestic and foreign-produced goods can be achieved through a trivial change in the exchange rate. If we also assume domestic and foreign bonds are perfect substitutes, the real rate of interest is set at the global level, and differences in national interest rates reflect only differences in expected rates of inflation. There are never any problems of financing a current account balance because investors can be induced to hold the required mix of domestic and foreign assets through a trivial change in relative yields. Through its assumptions the basic monetary model eliminates most issues of exchange rate determination.

The simple version of the monetary model has not performed well as an explanation of observed exchange rate movements. Its assumptions that PPP holds at all points in time and that domestic prices are sufficiently flexible to maintain continuous full employment also strike most analysts as too extreme. Subsequent models have gone on to explore the implications of relaxing the two key assumptions of perfect substitution between the demand for foreign and domestic goods and foreign and domestic bonds. They have attempted to maintain the assumption of PPP, however, as a plausible long-run condition defining an equilibrium exchange rate around which the actual rate fluctuates.

THE STICKY-PRICE MODEL. Rudiger Dornbusch explored the implications of the PPP assumption by eliminating it as a short-run condition while continuing to assume that it would hold in the long run.[8] If PPP does not hold at all points in time and domestic prices are sticky, an increase in the money supply, for example, could generate a less-than-proportionate rise in the price level, leading instead to an offsetting decline in the interest rate to absorb the excess balances. The result would be an emerging capital outflow and a depreciation of the exchange rate that is greater than would be expected from an equivalent change in the money supply within the flexible-price model. The depreciation must be greater so that there can be expectation of an exchange rate appreciation sufficient to cover the decline in the interest rate differential. Hence, in Dornbusch's model the exchange rate tends to overshoot the long-run response to a monetary change.

The sticky-price version can be illustrated by using ˜ to denote long-run equilibrium values.

$$(4\text{-}9) \qquad \tilde{e} = (\tilde{m} - \tilde{m}^*) - b_1(\tilde{y} - \tilde{y}^*) + b_2(\tilde{\pi} - \tilde{\pi}^*),$$

and by specifying that the exchange rate is expected to change in the future so as to eliminate a proportion, a, of the difference between the equilibrium and current rate in one period,

$$(4\text{-}10) \qquad \Delta e^e = a(\tilde{e} - e).$$

The current spot rate, e, can be obtained by again imposing interest rate parity,

$$(4\text{-}11) \qquad i - i^* = \Delta e^e = a(\tilde{e} - e),$$

so that

$$(4\text{-}12) \qquad e = \tilde{e} - 1/a\,(i - i^*).$$

The basic change from the flexible-price version lies in the addition of the negative coefficient on the interest rate differential. In fact, if $1/a$ exceeds b_2, the net coefficient on the interest rate term will be the opposite of that in equation 4-5 and will imply that a positive interest differential is associated with a currency appreciation.

Equation 4-12 is also a useful means of highlighting some of the problems that will be encountered in an empirical implementation of

8. Dornbusch (1976).

these disequilibrium models. The coefficient on the interest rate differential, $1/a$, is intended to measure the speed with which the exchange rate moves toward its equilibrium; but it also reflects the extent of disequilibrium. That is, a small interest rate differential (measured at annual rates) is consistent with a slow adjustment to a large disturbance or a fast adjustment to a small disturbance. If $1/a$ is to be a fixed parameter, the speed at which the exchange rate moves toward its equilibrium value must be independent of the original source of the disturbance, or all disturbances must be of equal size. It would seem only plausible that the market would view some disturbances as more permanent than others, and thus that the coefficient on the interest rate differential will be highly unstable over time.

PORTFOLIO-BALANCE MODELS. The implications of relaxing the second assumption of the monetary model, uncovered interest parity, are explored in a set of models that assume domestic and foreign bonds are imperfect substitutes and that resident investors have a greater preference than foreign investors for domestic assets.[9] Such models replace the interest rate parity assumption with an equation that relates the ratio of domestic to foreign bonds in investors' portfolios to the expected yield:

$$(4\text{-}13) \qquad (B/eB^*) = \lambda(i - i^* - (\Delta e)^e).$$

That is, investors are willing to increase the share of foreign assets in their portfolio only in response to a larger expected yield differential. To determine the level of the current exchange rate the portfolio model still requires some assumption, such as PPP, to specify the expected future or equilibrium exchange rate.

Jeffrey Frankel proposed a general exchange rate model that replaces the interest rate parity assumption of equation 4-11 with the imperfect substitution assumption of 4-13.[10] The result is

---

9. Portfolio models emphasize the allocation of domestic wealth among money, domestic assets, and foreign assets. Exclusive of capital gains, the total amount of wealth in each country is determined by domestic saving, but its allocation between domestic and foreign assets should be sensitive to relative rates of return. The monetary model assumes less-than-perfect substitution between money and other assets, but domestic and foreign bonds are perfect substitutes and can be treated as a single asset. Portfolio models assume that financial assets, other than money, are also imperfect substitutes for one another. A large number of studies concerned with portfolio models of the exchange rate are referenced in the article by Frankel (1983).

10. Frankel (1983), pp. 101–03.

$$(4\text{-}14) \qquad e = \beta_0(m - m^*) - \beta_1(y - y^*) - \\ \beta_2(i - i^*) + \beta_3(b - f),$$

where b and f are the logarithms of domestic and foreign bonds.

One problem in implementing the portfolio-balance models is that the appropriate measures of domestic and foreign assets depend on the currency in which the financial claims are denominated, and it is becoming increasingly common for governments and private firms to borrow in a foreign currency. However, it is possible to approximate eB^*/B with the negative of the cumulative sum of a country's current account expressed as a ratio to GDP or national wealth. Thus, a current account surplus implies a capital outflow, an increase in the net supply of foreign-denominated assets that must be held by domestic residents. If foreign bonds are an imperfect substitute for domestic bonds, their price must fall in terms of domestic currency to induce investors to hold them—which amounts to an exchange rate appreciation—or the interest rate spread must turn in favor of foreign bonds.[11]

The portfolio model is of interest because it suggests a mechanism by which developments in the current account would directly affect the exchange rate. Countries forced to borrow on a sustained basis in the international market would have to offer an increasing interest rate premium or suffer a depreciation of the exchange rate in relation to the expected future rate to induce foreign investors to increase the share of the borrowing country's debt in their portfolios. It also serves as a reminder that developments in exchange markets are likely to be dominated by changes in the supply of and demand for the stocks of foreign versus domestic assets, and those stocks are far larger than current account flows.

Real Exchange Rate Models

Because the various monetary models have been unable to explain the evolution of exchange rates over the 1980s—particularly the long cycle in the value of the dollar—attention has turned toward exchange rate models that incorporate real as well as monetary phenomena. Whereas the monetary models focused on the short-run dynamics of exchange rate adjustment about a long-term real rate that is assumed

11. This representation of the portfolio-balance model obviously is inappropriate in empirical models of bilateral exchange rates because it includes effects from third countries. It may be a useful approximation, however, for the models estimated in this volume for trade-weighted composite exchange rates.

to be fixed by purchasing power parity, more recent research has concentrated on that part of the change in the exchange rate that is attributable to shifts in investors' perceptions of the equilibrium or long-run exchange rate.

In part, the sticky-price model of Dornbusch, who rejected PPP as a short-run condition, was a precursor of this shift in emphasis. However, there are serious doubts about the value of PPP even as a long-run anchor for the exchange rate. Existing measures of real exchange rates appear to deviate widely from PPP for sustained periods of time; and empirical models of exports and imports are unable to obtain the large price elasticities that would be implied by PPP, even after allowing for lags extending over several years.[12] In exploring the implications of rejecting PPP, economists have developed another class of exchange rate models that focus on other determinants of the long-run or equilibrium exchange rate.

NOMINAL VERSUS REAL EXCHANGE RATES.   Although it is not essential to focus on the real exchange rate in order to consider real sector influences, such an approach simplifies the exposition and highlights some of the basic issues. The change is relatively easy to obtain through a combination of the uncovered interest rate parity condition and the definition of the real exchange rate. The real exchange rate is defined in logarithms as

$$(4\text{-}15) \qquad\qquad q = e + p^* - p,$$

and the nominal interest rate is decomposed into the real rate, r, and the expected annual inflation rate over the period T,

$$(4\text{-}16) \qquad\qquad i_T = r_T + \pi_T.$$

Using these definitions to replace the measures of the nominal exchange rate and nominal interest rate, the uncovered interest rate parity condition of equation 4-2 can be expressed as

12. The U.S. experience with an extreme change in the real exchange rate can be viewed as a test of the hypothesis that statistical estimates of trade price elasticities were biased downward. One can account for the change in the trade balance between 1980 and 1986 with trade elasticities of approximately unity. If the elasticities had been significantly larger, the change in the trade deficit should have been even greater than the huge deterioration experienced by the United States. If trade is 20 percent of GDP, the implied aggregate elasticity of substitution between domestic and foreign goods is only about 0.2, which is far too low to be consistent with an assumption that they are close substitutes.

$$(4\text{-}17) \qquad\qquad q = E(q_T) + r_T - r^*_T.$$

For example, the sticky-price model of equation 4-12 could be expressed in real terms as

$$(4\text{-}18) \qquad\qquad q = \bar{q} + 1/a \, (r - r^*).$$

The determinants of today's real exchange rate are reduced to two factors: an expected long-term or equilibrium value, plus a positive coefficient on the real interest rate differential, which is a measure of the extent of departure between the current and equilibrium rates and the speed with which the exchange rate is expected to move toward its equilibrium.

CURRENT ACCOUNT EQUILIBRIUM.   One means of including real sector influences is to modify the PPP definition of the expected future exchange rate to include changes in the trade balance. With imperfect substitution between domestic and foreign goods, there is a set of expected real exchange rates corresponding to different expected levels of the trade balance, rather than the single value obtained by strict adherence to PPP. These rates will be closely grouped if the elasticity of substitution between domestic and foreign goods is high and will be widely dispersed if it is low.

Several models then go on to impose the assumption of balance in the current account as an equilibrium condition, instead of PPP.[13] If changes in the current account balance can only be achieved at the cost of significant changes in the real exchange rate, and if the magnitude of that response to the real exchange rate is denoted by g, the deviation between the current and the equilibrium exchange rate can be specified as

$$(4\text{-}19) \qquad\qquad q - \bar{q} = NX/g,$$

where NX is the prevailing current account balance. The magnitude of the associated change in the exchange rate is then dependent on estimates of the sensitivity of trade flows to changes in relative prices. If price elasticities are low, the change in the real exchange rate required to return to equilibrium will be large. These models run into problems,

13. See Campbell and Clarida (1987) and Hooper and Morton (1982).

however, when they attempt to justify why balance in the current account should be imposed as an equilibrium or steady state condition.

Peter Hooper and John Morton incorporated the current account into the process by which investors form expectations of the equilibrium exchange rate without literally imposing a requirement of long-run balance.[14] Instead, they viewed investors as desiring to hold a diversified portfolio of foreign assets. In the long run the rate of net foreign asset accumulation—the current account—must be consistent with that stock equilibrium. Because wealth is steadily growing, there is room for a persistent current account imbalance sufficient to supply the net increment of foreign assets. In addition, Hooper and Morton used UIP as the mechanism for defining the adjustment path. The resulting model relates the real exchange rate to the cumulative past sum of the current account and the differential between domestic and foreign interest rates. Although the reasoning is somewhat different, the resulting specification is similar to the portfolio balance model.

GENERAL EQUILIBRIUM MODELS. Many general equilibrium models do not directly impose any long-run conditions on the exchange rate.[15] Instead, the equilibrium rate emerges out of the theoretical constraints imposed on other elements of the models. In particular, the equilibrium current account is obtained as the residual after balancing countries' expected future domestic saving and investment requirements. These conditions arise, in turn, out of various intertemporal conditions for maximizing utility. The steady-state exchange rate is then determined as the rate required to produce the specific current account balance. These models do require some means of specifying an adjustment path for the exchange rate in intermediate periods, however; and they typically do so by assuming UIP, linking changes in the exchange rate to interest rate differentials.

Empirical Analysis

This section explores the usefulness of the various exchange rate models to explain the actual behavior of the trade-weighted exchange rate for a sample of sixteen industrial countries. The countries are those used by Morgan Guaranty Trust Company (MG) to construct its data

14. Hooper and Morton (1982).
15. For example, McKibbin and Sachs (1991).

on effective exchange rates, and they differ from those used elsewhere in this study only by the addition of Switzerland and Spain and the exclusion of Finland. The Morgan Guaranty indexes are weighted averages of each country's exchange rate with its trading partners wherein the weights are the share of the trading partner in the country's total exports and imports.[16] Thus each country's exchange rate is expressed as a ratio to an average of its major competitors. Morgan Guaranty also publishes parallel measures of real exchange rates, where the nominal exchange rate is adjusted for differences in relative price levels. The real exchange rates are computed using producer prices exclusive of food and fuel. The use of a producer price index can be viewed as a compromise between using broader price indexes, such as those for GDP and consumer expenditures, which include many nontraded goods—particularly services—and a narrow index based on export or import prices that may be too reflective of the global market.[17]

The MG exchange rates produced the most satisfactory results in this and the following chapter, which focuses on the relationship between exchange rates and trade flows. It is important to note that the MG indexes of exchange rates are expressed as the foreign currency price of a unit of domestic currency. Thus, unlike the definition used in the preceding section, an increase in the index is associated with appreciation of the currency in question. The historical data for the effective nominal and real exchange rates are shown in appendix figures 4A-1 for each of the countries.

Most of the other data used in the following analysis are from sources such as the OECD and the International Monetary Fund (IMF). Variables used to explain changes in the exchange rate are constructed as the difference between the domestic value and the average of the competitor countries. The MG trade weights for each country were used to construct geometrically weighted averages of the data for the competitor countries. In the case of the money supply, price levels, and GDP,

16. The trade weights are modified on the export side to reflect the role of third countries in export markets. A more detailed description of the exchange rate indexes and the weights used for each country after 1983 can be found in Morgan Guaranty (1983, 1986). Although the weights used to construct the exchange rate indexes have changed slightly over time, I have used the post-1983 weights in the calculation of other variables.

17. The exclusion of food and fuel prices is important because they are strongly influenced by taxes and government controls. Domestic prices of these products often change in ways that do not reflect competitive positions in the global market. Their impact on production costs is still reflected in the prices of other products.

the variable used in the regressions is the logarithm difference between the specific country and the average of its competitors. In the case of interest rates, measures of price change, and the current account the competitor averages are based on arithmetic weighting. Unless otherwise noted, the regression estimates are based on quarterly data extending over the period 1973–90.

Nominal Exchange Rates

Regression estimates of the basic monetary model of the nominal exchange rate (see equation 4-5 in the preceding section) are shown in table 4-1. The most striking result is the extreme variability of the parameter estimates. For the MG indexes, positive coefficients should be identified with a currency appreciation. Thus we should expect a positive coefficient on the GDP variable and negative coefficients on the money supply and interest rate. The coefficients are perverse in sign, however, for seven countries in the case of GDP, three countries for the money supply, and six countries for the interest rate differential. In only seven of the sixteen equations do all three coefficients have the anticipated sign, and even in those cases the coefficients of relative money growth and GDP are far from the hypothesized values of unity. In addition, many of the equations have sizable average errors that display evidence of extreme autocorrelation. The monetary model does a particularly poor job of accounting for variations in the U.S. dollar exchange rate: all three coefficients are statistically significant, but perverse in sign.

Similar results were obtained for versions of the model that substituted differences in rates of inflation for the interest rate differential (see equation 4-8 of the preceding chapter), and they are not reported in detail.[18] Finally, an alternative set of regressions in which the estimation period was restricted to 1980–90 resulted in substantial changes in the results for individual countries; but, again, there was no general pattern of improvement in the performance of the model.

The general impression is that the estimates for the monetary model are extremely sensitive to the choice of countries, periods of estimation, and specific definitions of the variables used to represent the model. It is possible to obtain smaller average errors in the equations

18. Measures of relative inflation were constructed by using GDP price deflators, consumer prices, and the producer price index. The choice of the price index does change the results for individual countries, but there is no uniform pattern in which one specific index yielded superior results.

TABLE 4-1. *Performance of the Basic Monetary Model, Logarithms of Quarterly Data, 1973–90*

Country	Money supply	GDP	Interest rate	R^2	Standard error	Durbin-Watson
United States	1.24	− 5.12	0.059	0.60	0.07	0.48
	(8.76)	(6.92)	(8.32)			
Canada	− 0.04	− 2.04	− 0.012	0.60	0.07	0.10
	(0.41)	(5.08)	(0.59)			
Japan	− 1.69	2.59	0.002	0.81	0.13	0.20
	(3.86)	(9.23)	(0.19)			
Australia	− 0.74	1.89	− 0.076	0.82	0.12	0.29
	(4.73)	(1.69)	(9.04)			
Large European countries						
France	− 0.38	2.36	− 0.001	0.55	0.08	0.12
	(6.86)	(2.26)	(0.03)			
Germany	− 0.70	0.32	0.001	0.94	0.04	0.42
	(13.46)	(0.66)	(0.08)			
Italy	− 1.15	− 0.65	− 0.009	0.98	0.04	1.21
	(20.52)	(1.69)	(3.69)			
United Kingdom	− 0.17	2.28	− 0.020	0.50	0.10	0.16
	(− 6.24)	(4.02)	(− 2.27)			
Small European countries						
Austria	0.98	− 2.18	− 0.016	0.27	0.07	0.09
	(3.88)	(2.55)	(1.24)			
Belgium	0.17	− 0.07	0.004	0.15	0.06	0.08
	(1.93)	(0.13)	(0.41)			
Denmark	− 0.58	1.21	− 0.016	0.53	0.06	0.27
	(7.95)	(4.25)	(3.87)			
Netherlands	− 0.23	− 1.66	0.003	0.70	0.05	0.09
	(1.78)	(2.99)	(0.18)			
Norway	− 0.35	0.76	− 0.029	0.57	0.05	0.20
	(2.00)	(3.46)	(6.48)			
Spain	− 0.91	1.85	− 0.051	0.34	0.13	0.21
	(3.65)	(1.97)	(3.25)			
Sweden	− 0.90	1.44	− 0.053	0.84	0.07	0.78
	(6.68)	(3.53)	(7.29)			
Switzerland	− 0.90	− 1.37	0.005	0.91	0.07	0.24
	(7.89)	(3.48)	(0.75)			

SOURCES: Organization for Economic Cooperation and Development (1991b and 1992c) and author's calculations as explained in the text. T-statistics are in parentheses.

by correcting the data for autocorrelation, but the correction does not change the conclusion of substantial variability in the magnitude and sign of the individual coefficients.

The poor performance of the monetary model is consistent with many prior studies, and in general it is due to one of two hypotheses: there are substantial departures of exchange rates from PPP, or shifts in the underlying money demand functions result in poor predictions of the relative price levels. It is possible to distinguish between these two explanations by relating the nominal exchange rate directly to the ratio of the domestic and foreign price levels. Thus we can test the assumption of PPP by estimating the relationship between the nominal exchange rate and an independent measure of relative price levels.

Some simple tests of the correlation between the nominal exchange rate and relative prices are shown in table 4-2. Annual changes in the logarithm of the nominal exchange rate were regressed on changes in the ratio of the domestic to the trade-weighted foreign price index. The table shows the coefficients on the relative price term for the producer price index and consumer prices. By including a constant term, in the first-difference regressions we can evaluate the influence of relative prices in terms of their deviations from a constant trend rate of change.[19] Estimates of the relationship in levels with a correction for autocorrelation are shown in column three of the table.

The most striking result is the strong confirmation of the principal argument of the monetary model, namely, that there is an inverse relationship between the nominal exchange rate and relative price levels. Nearly all the coefficients have negative signs and many are surprisingly close to unity. In fact, using changes in producer prices, the hypothesis that the coefficient is equal to unity can be rejected for only six countries. While such an outcome would be obvious for a set of countries with high and variable inflation rates, the strength of the relationship is a surprise for this set of OECD countries, which have such similar long-term inflation rates. The coefficients are more closely clustered about a value of negative unity in the levels version, which effectively suppresses the trend term. A proportionate relationship between the nominal exchange rate and relative price levels is least evident for the United Kingdom and several of the smaller European countries.

---

19. There is no significant evidence for any country of a significant additional correlation with either lagged or future changes in relative prices.

TABLE 4-2. *Impact of Relative Prices on the Nominal Exchange Rate, Logarithms of Annual Data, 1973–90*

| Country | First differences in price coefficients | | Levels version[a] | |
	Producer prices	Consumer prices	Coefficient	Standard error
United States	−0.68	−0.64	−1.29	(0.89)
Canada	−1.11	−0.43	−1.47	(0.38)
Japan	−0.90	−0.34	−1.04	(0.13)
Australia	−1.42	−2.07[b]	−1.23	(0.13)
Large European countries				
France	−0.68	−1.72[b]	−0.89	(0.19)
Germany	−0.54	0.01[b]	−0.89	(0.09)
Italy	−1.09	−0.86	−0.94	(0.06)
United Kingdom	−0.21[b]	−0.21[b]	−0.50	(0.12)
Small European countries				
Austria	−0.30[b]	−0.02[b]	−0.54	(0.27)
Belgium	−0.72	−0.29[b]	−0.14	(0.22)
Denmark	0.43[b]	−1.05[b]	−0.22	(0.12)
Netherlands	0.04[b]	0.64[b]	−0.83	(0.18)
Norway	−0.53[b]	−0.64[b]	−0.63	(0.12)
Spain	−1.21	−1.30	−0.80	(0.09)
Sweden	−1.45	−0.57	−1.07	(0.14)
Switzerland	0.00[b]	−0.51	−1.17	(0.08)

SOURCE: Relative price indexes are constructed using the same weights as in the Morgan Guaranty exchange rate indexes.

a. The levels version is based on producer prices, and regressions are corrected for autocorrelation.

b. Denotes coefficients that are significantly different from a minus unity at the 95 percent confidence level.

These results suggest that the poor performance of the monetary model should not be attributed to a rejection of PPP. It appears, instead, that simple money demand functions do a relatively poor job of tracing out changes in countries' price levels and that relating the exchange rate to ratios of the determinants of the money demand function introduces a substantial degree of error. On the other hand, while the coefficients of the relative price term are consistent with the PPP hypothesis, variations in relative prices account for only a small proportion of the year-to-year variation in nominal exchange rates; the R^2 values of the annual first difference regressions are well below 50 percent, except for Italy, where the rate of domestic inflation has been far above that of its trading partners. Apparently PPP is important, but it is not everything.

The need to take into account relative price changes is also evident from a simple inspection of the path of the real and nominal exchange rates in figure 4A-1. Although the real rates are not completely free of trend and they vary sharply over the short term, they display substantially greater long-run stability than the indexes of nominal rates. There is a statistically significant trend in the nominal exchange rate over the period 1973–90 for fourteen of the sixteen countries under consideration. For thirteen of those countries, the conversion to a real exchange rate using producer prices reduces the magnitude of the trend, and it becomes insignificant for five countries.[20]

One notable problem is that the path of real exchange rates varies greatly, depending upon the choice of the price indexes that are used to make the adjustment for relative price inflation. For example, a comparison of producer prices indicates that Japan experienced a 52 percent decline in the relative price of its products between 1973 and 1990, whereas consumer prices put the figure at only 26 percent. For other countries the differences in implied rates of relative inflation are generally less than 10 percent over the span of seventeen years, but the differences are often substantial over shorter periods of time.

The choice of a specific price index was examined in greater detail by correlating annual changes in the nominal exchange rates with a broader range of alternative measures of relative price levels. These included, in addition to producer and consumer prices, GDP price deflators, export price deflators, and unit labor costs. The alternative measures of prices could be evaluated either in terms of the amount of residual variance or the closeness of the estimated coefficient to the value of unity hypothesized by PPP. However, there was a strong tendency for those equations with the smallest error to also produce the coefficient closest to unity. Thus it was enough to emphasize differences in the residual errors.

The indexes based on export prices and producer prices performed measurably better than those based on consumer prices, GDP prices, or unit labor costs. If the relative price indexes were ranked by overall goodness of fit for each country, for example, the average scores were export prices (1.7), producer prices (2.0), consumer prices (3.0), and GDP prices (3.3). Unit labor cost measures were not available for all

20. There is no significant trend in the nominal exchange rate for the United States and Belgium, and the conversion to a real exchange rate measure reverses the trend for the United Kingdom from a secular decline in the nominal rate to an increase in the real rate.

countries, but in general they performed poorly. These results are not so surprising because the first two measures come closest to measuring the prices of products that actually enter into international trade. The producer price index appears to provide the most reasonable basis for constructing a real exchange rate; but reliable measures of export prices were not available on a quarterly basis, and the export price indexes, by being influenced by competitors in the global market, may provide too little information about domestic cost trends. The differences in the correlation between changes in the nominal exchange rate and alternative measures of relative price trends were not enough, however, to eliminate all the ambiguity in constructing a measure of the real exchange rate.

Real Exchange Rates

The results of the preceding section support the argument put forth by Dornbusch and others that differences in secular inflation rates are important determinants of nominal exchange rates, but that rigidities in price adjustments leave room for substantial departures of the nominal interest rate about the level defined by PPP. Thus the subsequent analysis imposes a coefficient of unity on relative prices and focuses on changes in the real exchange rate.[21]

INTEREST-RATE DIFFERENTIALS. The sticky-price model, as shown in equation 4-18, provides the simplest representation of the real exchange rate. It implies that the expected equilibrium real exchange rate is a constant and assumes that UIP relates the deviations from equilibrium to differences between domestic and foreign interest rates.

Regressions were estimated by comparing the real exchange rate to several alternative measures of the difference between domestic and foreign interest rates. Those alternatives included short- and long-term nominal interest rates and constructed estimates of real interest rates. For short-term interest rates the inflation adjustment was based both on the actual rate of consumer price inflation one year ahead and on a five-quarter-centered moving average. There was little difference in the performance of the two alternatives, but the centered moving average

---

21. In a more formal test of this assumption, the real exchange rate regressions presented in table 4-4 were reestimated using the nominal exchange rate and including the ratio of the domestic and foreign price levels on the right-hand side. For twelve of the sixteen countries, the price coefficient did not differ significantly from − 1.0. The exceptions were Austria, Belgium, Denmark, and the Netherlands.

was chosen because it was a smoother adjustment that left intact more of the short-run variation in the nominal rate. The long-term real interest rate was constructed using both a twelve-quarter-centered average of consumer price changes and an alternative that incorporated much longer trends of past inflation.[22] Although the differences were again relatively minor, the measure based on long-run inflation trends performed somewhat better and was used in all the reported analyses. The interest-rate differentials were constructed using the MG weights to compute an average of the foreign interest rates.

A representative set of regressions based on the differential in long-term real interest rates is shown in table 4-3. The dependent variable is the logarithm of the MG real exchange rate, and a trend term is included to correct for any error in the measurement of the trend in the real exchange rate. The overall results are quite disappointing; in nearly half the cases the coefficient on the interest rate differential is negative, and a significant positive coefficient could be obtained for only five countries. For the G-7 economies, the common view, arising out of models that assume UIP, that a rise in the domestic interest rate in relation to foreign rates will have a positive impact on the exchange rate, is strongly confirmed only for the U.S. dollar. The regressions also continue to display a high degree of autocorrelation in the residuals.

One finding is that, despite the difficulties of adjusting for expected inflation, measures of international differences in real interest rates are nearly always preferred to the nominal rate differentials. In addition, the statistical significance of the interest rate differential is generally greater for those differentials constructed on the basis on the long-term bond rate. Short-term interest rates are far more volatile than long-term rates, but much of that variation does not appear to be reflected in the exchange rate. In a few European countries, however, the short-term interest rates show a closer correlation with the exchange rate. That result may reflect the thin nature of some of the European long-term bond markets and strong government control over credit for much of the period under analysis.

22. The long-term expected inflation rate was constructed using a survey of expected inflation in the United States over a ten-year horizon, as reported by financial market participants to Drexel Burnham for the period 1979–89. A regression model was used to relate the expected rate to actual inflation rates. The best fit was obtained by viewing the expected rate as a weighted average of the short run (represented by the twelve-quarter-centered moving average of consumer price inflation) and the long run (the average inflation rate over the preceding ten years). The long-run component was assigned a weight of 70 percent. The formula was then used to calculate expected inflation for all the countries in the sample.

TABLE 4-3. *Regression Equations for the Real Exchange Rate and Interest Rate Differentials, Logarithms of Quarterly Data, 1973–90*

Country	Interest rate differential	Time trend	R^2	Standard error	Durbin-Watson
United States	6.57	a	0.49	0.08	0.3
	(8.3)				
Canada	1.67	−0.17	0.32	0.05	0.1
	(1.2)	(5.5)			
Japan	1.41	a	0.03	0.10	0.2
	(1.4)				
Australia	−4.02	a	0.29	0.08	0.3
	(5.3)				
Large European countries					
France	−3.75	−0.14	0.44	0.04	0.3
	(4.9)	(5.9)			
Germany	1.54	a	0.12	0.04	0.3
	(3.1)				
United Kingdom	−3.94	0.41	0.85	0.06	0.3
	(11.6)	(11.8)			
Italy	−0.77	0.06	0.33	0.03	0.4
	(3.5)	(3.7)			
Small European countries					
Austria	1.88	0.30	0.94	0.02	0.7
	(6.2)	(33.0)			
Belgium	0.83	−0.69	0.89	0.05	0.1
	(1.5)	(21.7)			
Denmark	−0.85	a	0.08	0.06	0.1
	(2.4)				
Netherlands	3.18	−0.08	0.19	0.04	0.6
	(3.8)	(2.3)			
Norway	0.89	a	0.18	0.03	0.3
	(4.0)				
Spain	1.60	a	0.17	0.06	0.2
	(3.2)				
Sweden	−3.02	a	0.27	0.05	0.3
	(5.1)				
Switzerland	0.13	0.12	0.15	0.06	0.3
	(0.2)	(3.4)			

SOURCES: The dependent variable is the logarithm of the Morgan Guaranty real exchange rate. The interest rate differential is based on the long-term real interest rates defined in the text. All coefficients are rescaled by 100. T-statistics are in parentheses.

a. Variable excluded from regression.

PORTFOLIO-BALANCE EFFECTS. A final test was to examine the performance of the portfolio-balance model, which assumes that domestic and foreign bonds are imperfect substitutes and rejects uncovered interest rate parity. As discussed previously, the cumulative sum of the current account, expressed as a percentage of GDP, is used as an estimate of the net supply of claims on foreigners (positive or negative) that must be absorbed in financial markets. Investors can be induced to hold an increased supply of foreign claims either through a reduction in the domestic interest rate in relation to the yield in other countries, or through an exchange rate appreciation that reduces the current price of those foreign assets and thereby creates greater expectation of a future capital gain. Hooper and Morton also included the variable in their model, where they interpreted it as a determinant of the expected future exchange rate. Net changes in official government reserves were deducted from the current account in order to focus on changes in private claims. The flow data were then cumulated over the period 1970—90 to obtain an estimate of the net stock of claims.[23]

Table 4-4 shows a representative set of equations in which the cumulative sum of the current account is an added explanatory variable. The dependent variable is the logarithm of the MG real exchange rate, and the regressions are estimated using annual data over the period 1973-90. The annual frequency was adopted for this final set of equations because it sharply reduces the problem of autocorrelation of the residuals. A clear positive relationship emerges between the lagged value of the cumulative sum of the current account, expressed as a ratio to GDP, and the exchange rate. It appears for thirteen of the sixteen countries. In addition, the fit of the equations improved substantially after government reserves were deducted from the measure of net claims on foreigners.

It is still difficult, however, to obtain a consistent result for interest rates. First, there is evidence of a positive relationship between the exchange rate and the interest differential for eight countries (United States, France, Germany, Italy, Austria, Belgium, Denmark, and the Neth-

---

23. Because an estimate of the initial net stock of foreign assets is not available, it was set to zero at the beginning of 1970. This treatment introduces a false trend in the ratio of net claims to GDP, the formulation that is actually used in the regressions. It provides another reason, in addition to the uncertainty in measuring the trend of the real exchange rate, for including a time trend in the regressions. In fact, the statistical significance of the trend variable is largely associated with the inclusion of the cumulative sum in the regressions, rather than reflecting any substantial trend in the real exchange rate.

TABLE 4-4. *Regression Equations for the Real Exchange Rate, Annual Data, 1973–90*

Country	Cumulative sum of the current account	Interest differential	Time trend	R^2	Standard error	Durbin-Watson
United States	3.36	3.94	7.68	0.86	0.04	1.9
	(5.0)	(3.3)	(5.1)			
Canada	1.10	1.33	[a]	0.63	0.04	1.0
	(5.0)	(0.5)				
Japan	1.30	2.41[b]	[a]	0.54	0.06	1.7
	(3.5)	(2.5)				
Australia	1.75	1.80	2.92	0.67	0.06	1.6
	(3.6)	(0.6)	(2.5)			
Large European countries						
France	2.21	2.40[c]	[a]	0.46	0.04	1.1
	(3.0)	(3.0)				
Germany	0.59	0.93[c]	[a]	0.49	0.03	1.4
	(3.1)	(3.2)				
United Kingdom	0.54	−4.28	1.68	0.91	0.05	1.2
	(1.7)	(6.6)	(6.9)			
Italy	0.83	0.82[c]	[a]	0.57	0.02	1.4
	(4.2)	(3.6)				
Small European countries						
Austria	[a]	2.25	1.22	0.96	0.01	1.8
		(3.9)	(19.0)			
Belgium	0.56	2.43	−2.02	0.98	0.03	1.6
	(6.9)	(3.9)	(11.8)			
Denmark	0.57	0.91[c]	0.82	0.52	0.05	1.3
	(2.4)	(2.1)	(1.8)			
Netherlands	0.31	4.77	−0.95	0.39	0.03	1.5
	(1.5)	(2.7)	(2.3)			
Norway	[a]	[a]	0.41	0.38	0.03	1.3
			(3.1)			
Spain	1.16	0.15	[a]	0.72	0.04	1.8
	(4.1)	(0.2)				
Sweden	0.40	0.77[c]	0.61	0.57	0.04	1.2
	(3.0)	(1.1)	(1.5)			
Switzerland	[a]	0.79[c]	0.58	0.22	0.06	1.5
		(1.0)	(2.0)			

SOURCES: The dependent variable is the logarithm of the Morgan Guaranty real exchange rate. Other variables are defined in the text. Unless otherwise noted, the interest rate differential is based on the long-term real rates. All coefficients are rescaled by 100. T-statistics are in parentheses.

a. Variable excluded from regression.

b. For Japan, the domestic interest rate is statistically insignificant and the coefficient is based solely on the U.S. long-term rate.

c. Differential in short-term interest rates.

erlands). Even within this group a positive coefficient could be obtained only by varying the definition of the appropriate interest rate, using the short-term real rate for France, Germany, Italy, and Denmark, and the long-term real rate for the others. The model works particularly well in accounting for variations in the value of the dollar. The equation predicts nearly all of the 33 percent rise in the trade-weighted exchange rate between 1980 and 1984, and it captures a large proportion of the decline over the last half of the 1980s; but there is a large 7 percent error in 1985 when the predicted rate fell sharply. A better-fitting equation could be obtained for Germany by replacing the interest differential with the German and U.S. rates entered separately. The problem is that the positive coefficient on the German interest rate has a magnitude of only one-fourth that of the negative coefficient on the U.S. rate.

More serious problems were encountered in the exchange rate equations for Japan and the United Kingdom. In the case of Japan, there is a significant negative relationship with foreign interest rates, but no evidence of any positive association with domestic interest rates. The results for the United Kingdom are even more perplexing. There is a highly significant negative correlation between the exchange rate and the interest rate differential. If the domestic and foreign interest rates are entered separately, both are highly significant, but with perverse signs. The U.S. interest rate is responsible for most of the negative influence of foreign rates, and the results are robust for a wide variety of alternative interest rate measures[24] The equations for both the United Kingdom and Japan also have large residual errors, which indicate major movements in their exchange rates that are unexplained by the present model.

There is weak evidence of a positive correlation with interest rate differentials for Canada, Australia, Spain, Sweden, and Switzerland. Norway stands out as the one country for which the exchange rate does not correlate with either interest rates or the current account balance.

A possible reason for the failure to obtain a positive coefficient on the interest rate differential for some countries is that the regression equations reflect the response of governments rather than private investors. If the monetary authorities target the exchange rate, they may respond to a perceived weakness of the exchange rate by adopting a

---

24. This result is contradicted in a recent paper by Fisher and his colleagues (1990), who found a positive relationship for the United Kingdom. In the current context, however, their suggestion that the actual future exchange rate should be included as a proxy for the expected rate did not alter the perverse sign on the interest rate differential.

higher domestic interest rate to attract foreign capital. As a result, the sign of the simple correlation between interest rates and the exchange rate would be the opposite of that expected on the basis of private investors' behavior. It suggests that the behavior of governments needs to be incorporated into the model of exchange rate determination; but this issue is not explored further in this analysis.

The switch from quarterly to annual data was motivated by problems with autocorrelation in the residuals of the quarterly regressions. If an effort is made to reduce the autocorrelation by transforming the quarterly data, the variance in the real exchange rate becomes very small, leaving little to be explained. But the regressions based on annual data do not show evidence of autocorrelation in their residuals. Autocorrelation appears to be an important property of the data only in the very short run. At the same time, estimation of the equations of table 4-4 using quarterly data has little effect on the coefficients of either the cumulative sum of the current account or interest rate differentials. This result is consistent with the view that exchange rates are influenced over intervals of a year or longer by basic economic forces, such as interest differentials, relative rates of price change, and current account developments; but in the short run the changes are dominated by expectations of investors, which in turn appear to be dominated by extrapolations of recent trends. Those short-run elements are inherently difficult to model empirically. Nonetheless, a significant proportion of the annual variation in the exchange rate remains unexplained by the variables included in the regressions.

THE ROLE OF EXTERNAL SHOCKS.   Many recent explanations for the difficulties encountered in empirical studies of exchange rates have emphasized the role of events that alter investors' judgment of the equilibrium long-run rate. An example is provided by the sharp variations in oil prices in 1973, 1979, and 1986. Oil-importing countries had to dramatically increase their non-oil trade surplus to pay the increased cost of oil imports, and the mechanism for accomplishing this should have been a decline in their real exchange rates. For the four countries in the sample that are significant energy exporters (Canada, the Netherlands, Norway, and the United Kingdom) a rise in energy prices might be expected to have a positive effect on the real exchange rate.[25] As a

---

25. Of course, the effects on the perceived equilibrium rate would be affected by investors' beliefs about the permanence of the oil price changes.

test of the hypothesis, the equations of table 4-4 were reestimated with an additional variable defined as net exports of energy expressed as a share of GDP. An alternative specification used the price of oil. The coefficients were statistically insignificant for the four energy exporters, and there was no systematic impact on the exchange rates of energy importers. The coefficient on the net trade balance in energy varied in both sign and magnitude and was statistically significant only for Germany, Italy, Denmark, and Sweden. A similar result was obtained when an index of nonfuel commodity prices was included in the exchange rate equations for Australia and Canada. In sum, these tests provide little evidence that countries' real exchange rates are altered in a systematic fashion by major global events or changed prices for their major exports.

It is possible that the statistical results have been greatly distorted by the changes in government regulations, which permitted a much greater degree of international capital mobility in the 1980s in relation to the 1970s. Because of the limited number of observations, it is difficult to test the stability of the parameters of the regressions based on annual data. However, the quarterly versions were reestimated for two subperiods of 1973–85 and 1978–90. The shortening of the data period does give rise to substantial instability in the parameter estimates. More important, there was no tendency for the overall fit of the equations to improve in the later period; nor was there any consistent evidence of an increased role for interest rate changes. For example, the lack of a positive correlation with the interest rate differential continues to be characteristic of the regressions for the British and Japanese exchange rates for a variety of different time periods and alternative interest rate definitions.

The equations of table 4-4 can also be evaluated by comparing the residual errors with those that would be obtained from a simple regression of the exchange rate on its own past value—which is essentially a forecast of no change. Using quarterly data, none of the equations produce a standard error smaller than the simple forecasting model. This result is similar to the conclusion of Richard Meese and Kenneth Rogoff, who found that the structural equations have no forecasting value. For most purposes, however, the importance of exchange rates lies in changes lasting longer than one quarter. If the same test is performed using the annual versions of the equations, the standard errors of the structural equations for nine of the sixteen countries are smaller than those of the simple model. This is principally the result of much larger residual errors in the annual version of the naive model. Except for the United States, the gains are not large; thus, even over periods as long as a year, a substantial proportion of the variance in real exchange rates remains unexplained.

Conclusion

Despite the emphasis in the current literature on the failure of PPP to hold in its most rigid form, differences in the rates of domestic price inflation emerge in this analysis as the most consistently important determinant of changes in nominal exchange rates. In particular, the adjustment for differences in domestic price inflation eliminates much of the evidence of any secular trend in exchange rates. The difficulty with PPP is not that it is wrong, but that it is only part of the story: the exchange rates of most industrial countries still show substantial variation in real terms. In addition, there is evidence that interest rate differentials are an important part of the explanation for exchange rate variations for some countries, particularly the United States. In the case of several countries, however, the failure to find a significant positive correlation with the interest rate differential remains puzzling. Third, the finding of a significant role for the cumulative sum of the current account is consistent with arguments that domestic and foreign assets are still far from perfect substitutes in investors' portfolios and thus that the interest parity assumption should be rejected. But as Hooper and Morton demonstrated, it could also be rationalized as being consistent with less-than-complete adherence to PPP in the long run. Fourth, the exchange rate model works well for the United States; but the United States does seem something of a special case in the empirical analysis. Thus empirical studies should avoid too much emphasis on exchange rates involving the dollar as the basis for testing alternative theories. The experience of other countries has been quite different.

For most countries a significant amount of variance in the exchange rate remains unexplained, in part because of short-term fluctuations, as reflected in a smaller residual variance for the equations estimated using annual data. In large part, however, it is the result of more fundamental movements. There are two potential explanations that are not adequately tested by this analysis. First, the substantial residual errors, together with the failure to find the strong interest rate effects implied by UIP, could be the result of an inadequate specification of the expected equilibrium rate. An effort was made to identify some events, such as changes in oil prices, that might be expected to alter expectations, and to test for a correlation with the exchange rate. Those results were not encouraging. Alternatively, the problems could be due to inadequate specification of the process of adjustment to an equilibrium rate. It is true that the model works well for the United States, which has long had open capital markets; and the vast change in the regulations of other countries may have strong distorting effects on the data. These problems remained unresolved, however, even when the data period was shortened to focus on the events of the 1980s.

FIGURE 4A-1. *Real and Nominal Exchange Rates, Sixteen Countries, 1970–90*

1980–82 average = 100

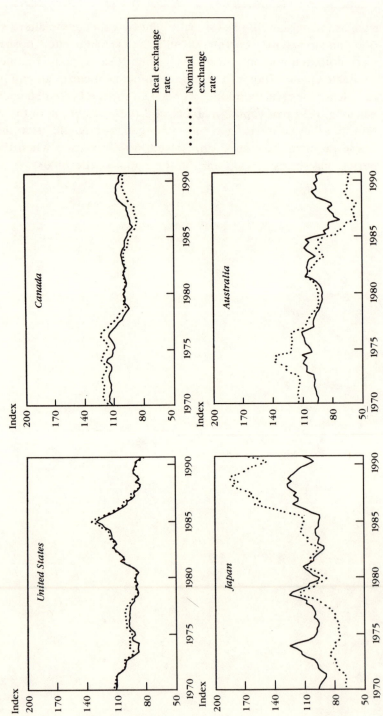

FIGURE 4A-1. (cont'd)

1980–82 average = 100

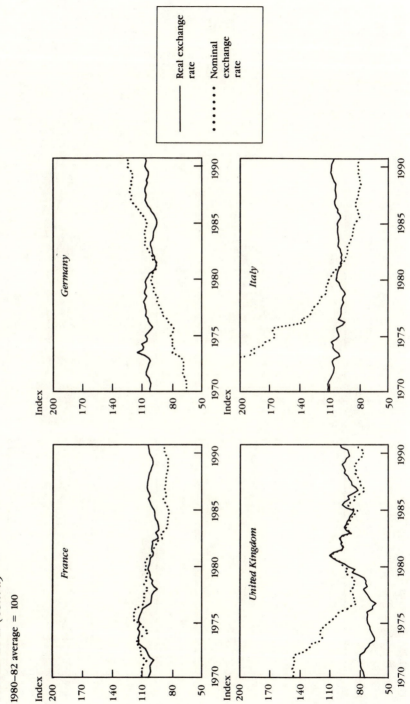

FIGURE 4A-1. (cont'd)
1980–82 average = 100

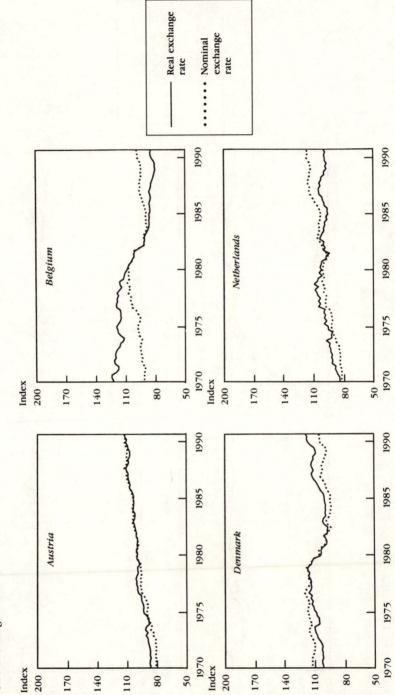

FIGURE 4A-1. *(cont'd)*
1980–82 average = 100

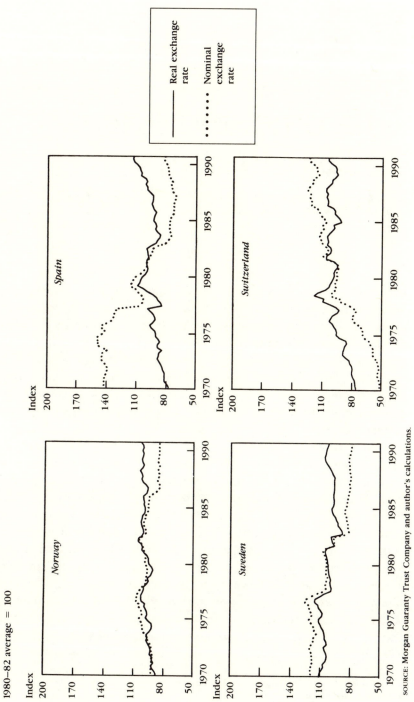

SOURCE: Morgan Guaranty Trust Company and author's calculations.

5

Income and Price Elasticities in International Trade

Despite all the attention that economists have devoted to real exchange rates in the debate over alternative policies to reduce current account imbalances, they remain surprisingly divided on the question of the actual importance of exchange rates as determinants of exports and imports. The argument in this volume is that variations in real exchange rates are an integral part of the process by which the external balance is realigned with a changed domestic balance of saving and investment. Thus in chapter 3 the determinants of the current account were examined from the perspective of the domestic saving-investment balance. Now it is time to consider the process by which changes in the domestic balance are reflected in the external balance, namely, through changes in incomes and relative prices.

During the 1980s it became fashionable to be an "elasticity pessimist," which meant providing reasons to expect trade flows to be unresponsive to changes in the relative price of domestic versus foreign goods. This pessimism arose in response to the small initial adjustment in the U.S. current account that occurred after 1985 in the face of what was perceived to be large changes in the value of the dollar. Some therefore advocated a managed-trade policy, arguing that the existing adjustment process was not working because the exports and imports of some countries, such as Japan, are insensitive to exchange rate changes. The exports and imports of these economies, it was alleged, are controlled by strategic goals of trade policy rather than prices in the market.[1]

---

1. There is a legitimate debate with Japan over the openness of its markets to imports; but absent changes in the domestic saving-investment balance, a higher level of Japanese

In addition, it was said that some exporters offset the effect of exchange rate changes by "pricing to market," that is, by adjusting their profit margins so as to maintain their prices in large markets such as the United States. Because of adjustments in capacity and costs of entry into foreign markets, the argument went, the effects of exchange rate increases and declines are not symmetric: once domestic producers have lost out to foreigners through an appreciation of the real exchange rate, a simple reversal of the prior increase is not enough to restore their market share.[2]

At the opposite extreme are those who favor the monetary approach to exchange rate determination, seeing changes in real exchange rates as a relatively incidental part of the adjustment process.[3] In their view domestic and foreign-produced goods are very good substitutes, and the price elasticities of exports and imports are so high that modest changes in real exchange rates will induce large realignments of the trade balance. Furthermore, because domestic prices are relatively flexible and easily altered by small changes in demand, there is no need to rely on changes in the nominal exchange rate to change the real exchange rate. Hence, in explaining the evolution of trade imbalances it is enough to focus on changes in the domestic saving-investment balance; a highly integrated international system for trade in goods and services will ensure the smooth transfer of any domestic surplus or deficit into the global market. Because this group believes in high price elasticities, it takes purchasing power parity (PPP) to be the key determinant of exchange rates in its analysis of the balance of payments.

Between these two extremes are those who believe that changes in relative prices have a substantial effect on trade, but this effect is not so large as to render trivial the changes in real exchange rates required to achieve variations in trade balances of the magnitude observed in the industrial economies. While agreeing with the monetary school that expenditure-reducing policies to alter the domestic balance of saving and investment are a prerequisite to effective adjustment, they also argue that rigidities in the realignment of trade flows and the adjustment of domestic prices make it equally important to develop

---

imports would be matched by even greater exports and little change in the trade balance. This distinction is often overlooked in the political debate, and thus some Americans perceive a more open Japanese market as a solution to the U.S. trade deficit.

2. The various reasons for expecting trade to respond relatively weakly to variations in real exchange rates are treated at greater length in Krugman and Baldwin (1987) and Krugman (1989), pp. 36–75.

3. McKinnon (1984), p. 72, and Mundell (1991).

policies that facilitate the transfer of resources through changes in the exchange rate. Relying on domestic price inflation or deflation alone to achieve the required magnitude of change in the relative price of domestic versus foreign-produced goods would be very costly.

By adopting the appropriate mix of fiscal and monetary policies, governments can speed the process of adjustment with considerably less disruption to the domestic economy than would otherwise be necessary. One possible mix would be a more restrictive fiscal policy and a less restrictive monetary policy. This fiscal move would free up domestic resources, while the monetary policy would induce a decline in interest rates and the exchange rate and thus speed the transfer of those resources into foreign markets.

The sensitivity of trade flows to variations in relative prices is thus a vital factor to consider in the debate over the need for expenditure-switching policies and the role of the flexible exchange rate system in the adjustment mechanism. If it were true that the elasticity of substitution between domestic and foreign goods is large, the monetarists would be correct in arguing that expenditure-switching is a minor part of the story, safely ignored in a focus on the need to realign domestic saving and investment. Having observed the large magnitude of swings in the American exchange rate during the 1980s, however, few economists would take seriously the claim of a high price elasticity.

The more serious challenge to the existing system comes from those who argue that adjustments of the exchange rate have only small effects on trade and are too costly a means of altering trade balances. Residents of a country experiencing a sharp fall in the real exchange rate do suffer a decline in their standard of living in that the goods they produce are worth less in relation to the cost of the goods they buy from others; that is, they suffer a decline in the terms of trade. The smaller the price elasticity of both exports and imports, the larger the losses required to achieve a given readjustment of the trade balance. A finding of a low price elasticity will thus inevitably lead people to call for more interventionist government policies toward trade as a means of avoiding real income losses.

Before the large fluctuations in the value of the dollar in the 1980s, most international trade economists interpreted the empirical evidence as suggesting that over a span of two or more years the sum of the price elasticities for exports and imports was well above unity. These values satisfied the Marshall-Lerner condition and implied that expenditure-switching policies are an effective part of the trade-balance adjustment.[4] However, lags in the adjustment to changes in relative prices were long enough to create perverse short-run responses of the trade balance to exchange rate movements.

Second, income elasticities were generally much higher, in the range of one to two for both exports and imports. The elasticities, however, often differed significantly between the import and export sides of the trade account, and they varied widely across countries.

At the same time, there were several reasons to be skeptical about the reliability of the estimated price and income elasticities. Even now, most empirical estimates are derived within a highly simplified framework. The volume of exports is related to an index of global economic activity, and the relative cost of domestic versus foreign goods expressed in a common currency. Similarly, the volume of imports is related to domestic economic activity and relative prices. In logarithms,

$$(5\text{-}1) \qquad X = a_0 + b_1 Y_f - b_2 (P_d/eP_f)$$

$$(5\text{-}2) \qquad M = a_1 + b_3 Y_d + b_4 (P_d/eP_f).$$

This formulation commingles the determinants of the supply and demand for both exports and imports. One rationalization is to assume that the price elasticity of supply is extremely high and interpret the equations as representing demand relationships. This might be a defensible argument in the case of imports if a country can draw from a large global market. On the export side, however, several authors have argued that supply constraints could lead analysts to underestimate the long-run price elasticities.[5]

On the other hand, several authors have argued that those empirical analyses that use actual import and export prices to measure the price elasticities overstate the effectiveness of exchange rate changes. The passthrough of exchange rate changes into import and export prices may be incomplete because exporters systematically adjust their prices to absorb a portion of any exchange rate change. Thus, the impact of exchange rate changes on trade flows is less than implied by a simple application of the price elasticities.

---

4. Goldstein and Khan (1985).
5. For a thorough survey and critique of the empirical estimates, together with an extensive discussion of the major econometric issues, see Goldstein and Kahn (1985). The issue of supply effects is examined for the United States in Hooper (1988).

Furthermore, most empirical studies obtain estimates of the income elasticities that are surprisingly high and widely varying among countries.[6]

Income elasticities above unity imply that trade should be a rising share of national output. Although that is true for the post-World War II period, the trend is not evident over longer periods of time; nor does the total output of the tradable goods industries appear to represent a rising share of GDP in the industrial countries.[7] It is not obvious why imports should constitute a rising share of income if the market basket of which they are a component is not. The growth of income might be reflected in a preference for a more diverse range of goods and increased imports in small economies, but there is no particular association between the size of the income elasticity and the size of the economy. Furthermore, the notion that the growth of trade is due to a high income elasticity ignores the positive contribution of the secular liberalization of trade over the past several decades. The general discussion of the growth of international trade has emphasized the importance of liberalization under the General Agreement on Tariffs and Trade (GATT). Yet, most of the empirical work attributes the growth of trade to the general expansion of the global economy. Some studies have made use of tariff rates as an index of trade restrictions; but they ignore changes in quotas and other quantitative restrictions, which have frequently been of greater importance.

In addition, the high income elasticities would seem to imply that countries with differing growth rates should have very different trade balances or divergent trends in their terms of trade. Fast-growing countries should have trade deficits, unless offset by a secular decline in real exchange rates. In practice, this pattern is not evident because rapidly growing countries, such as Japan, are found to have much higher income elasticities for exports than for imports; whereas the situation is just the opposite for slow-growing countries, such as the United States. The issue of unequal income elasticities for exports and imports was first raised by Hendrick Houthakker and Stephen Magee, who interpreted it

6. For recent empirical analyses of pass-through for the United States, see Hooper and Mann (1989) and Lawrence (1990).

7. For example, manufacturing, which is often used as a rough index of the tradable goods industries, is a relatively stable share of GDP in constant prices and is declining in nominal terms in most OECD countries. Long-term trends in trade ratios are explored in Gagnon and Rose (1990).

in the context of a trade balance constraint on growth: Japan could grow faster than other countries because the income elasticity for its exports was higher than for its imports.[8] More recently, Paul Krugman reversed the causation, arguing that rapid growth leads to a high income elasticity for exports because of increasing returns and product diversification.[9] Thus, the income elasticities in equations 5-1 and 5-2 are not fixed constants; rather, they vary systematically with growth. The magnitude of the income elasticity takes on added importance because several studies report that variations in the estimated income elasticity also have pronounced implications for the estimate of the price elasticity.

All of these concerns received increased attention in the mid-1980s, when the U.S. trade deficit failed to decline as rapidly as many analysts had predicted. A large number of new empirical studies were undertaken to re-estimate the income and price elasticities of U.S. trade with the data of the 1980s. In general, these studies concluded that the performance of U.S. trade during the 1980s could be explained by conventional models with estimates of the income and price elasticities similar to those obtained from the pre-1980 data. The principal change was that greater attention was paid to the lags in the adjustment process: both in the adjustment of traded-goods prices to exchange rate changes and in the response of trade flows to changes in prices.

Meanwhile, the reasons that the U.S. trade balance failed to fully reverse itself over the 1980s remained in dispute. Although the real exchange rate returned to the levels of 1980 by the end of the decade, the United States continued to run a trade deficit of about $100 billion in merchandise trade.[10] Could this state of affairs be due to a Houthakker-Magee effect in which the income elasticity of U.S. imports is simply higher than the global elasticity of demand for its exports, as argued by Robert Lawrence; to supply-side limitations that bias the estimates

8. For a more detailed discussion, see Johnson (1958) and Houthakker and Magee (1969). As a simple test of the relationship between the trade deficit and economic growth, the average trade balance of each of the fourteen industrial countries used in the following analysis was related to the average growth in GDP and the change in the real exchange rate for the periods 1965–80 and 1965–90. While the size of the sample is small, there was no significant correlation between growth and trade deficits for either period.

9. Krugman (1989b).

10. Lawrence (1990). His explanation emphasized the higher income elasticity for imports than for U.S. exports at a time when the growth of U.S. GDP was about the same as the average of its trading partners.

of long-run price responses, as argued by Peter Hooper; or to some notion of a secular decline in competitiveness, independent of the rate of growth of income?[11]

Most of the recent research has focused on the behavior of U.S. trade and has said little about the adjustment process in other countries. Yet, the wide range of fluctuation in real exchange rates during the 1980s offers a much richer set of data with which to investigate the magnitude of the price and income elasticities. As in previous chapters, the use of data from several countries provides a more robust evaluation of some of the conclusions obtained from earlier statistical analyses of U.S. trade behavior. Such data also provide a means of evaluating the experience with adjustment during the 1980s from a broader perspective than the United States alone. Did the system perform as badly as its critics charge? Was the reduction in trade imbalances less than we would have expected, given the changes in exchange rates and domestic economic policies that occurred?

The data on trade flows were obtained from the OECD national accounts for the period 1970–90.[12] The data were adjusted in two respects. First, the analysis excludes trade in energy. The countries in the sample vary substantially in the extent to which they rely on imported energy, and some are significant oil exporters. The sharp variations in oil prices obscure much of the underlying change in trade flows.

Second, the U.S. data were adjusted to exclude trade in computing equipment. The United States employs a price index for computers that has declined rapidly over the 1980s to construct a measure of trade volumes, using the price weights of a single base period. The combination of a single base period and large changes in the relative prices of the components has a dramatic effect on the index of trade volume changes.[13] For example, over the 1980–90 period the volume of manufactured exports, including computers, rose by 96 percent, compared with only 48 percent when computers are excluded. This difference arises despite the fact that the share of computers in the nominal value of manufacturing exports rose from 6 percent in 1980 to only 8.5 percent in 1990, and that the measures of export growth in nominal

11. See Hooper (1988); Hooper and Mann (1989); and Lawrence (1990).
12. The list of countries is basically the same as that in chapters 3 and 4, but there is some variation in the choice of small European countries because of data availability. For example, Switzerland and Finland are excluded completely, and it was not possible to obtain meaningful results for the nonenergy exports of Norway.
13. This issue is discussed in greater detail in Lawrence (1990).

prices are virtually identical, inclusive or exclusive of computers. The problem is less acute for other countries because computers form a smaller share of their trade, and most do not make use of the same price index. Their measures of traded-goods prices are not as dominated by pricing developments in a small component of trade. Because the United States is a major trading partner for most of the countries in this sample, the adjustment does, however, affect all the measures of relative traded goods prices.

Regressions were also estimated for trade in manufactured goods, as well as for total trade excluding energy. Although this study is primarily concerned with the behavior of aggregate trade flows, a parallel analysis using manufactures provided a check on some of the results.

The form of the estimated regression equations is similar to that used in recent studies of U.S. trade.[14] However, an effort was made to explore in more detail the source of the variation across countries in the magnitude of the income elasticities for both exports and imports. In addition, several measures of the relative price of traded goods were tested to determine the sensitivity of the results to alternative price concepts.

The next section provides a brief overview of the historical trend in trade balances for the leading economies. It is followed by a discussion of the regression estimates for exports and imports. Then the results for exports and imports are analyzed for their implications for the overall balance of nonenergy trade.

Historical Trends

Figure 5-1 presents the historical data on the overall trade balance and on nonenergy trade (expressed as a percentage of net domestic product) for the United States, Japan, Germany, and a European aggregate. Note the importance of energy imports in the trade balance. Although the United States began to run a trade deficit in the mid-1970s, it continued to have a significant surplus in nonenergy trade until 1983. Most other industrial countries depend on imported energy far more than the United States does, and they have had to obtain large surpluses on nonenergy trade to pay for their oil imports.

The fluctuations in energy trade balances are important because they drive a wedge between the balance as determined by domestic saving

---

14. See Lawrence (1990) and the citations included there.

FIGURE 5-1. *Trade Balance for Four Industrialized Economies, 1965–90*

Percent of net domestic product

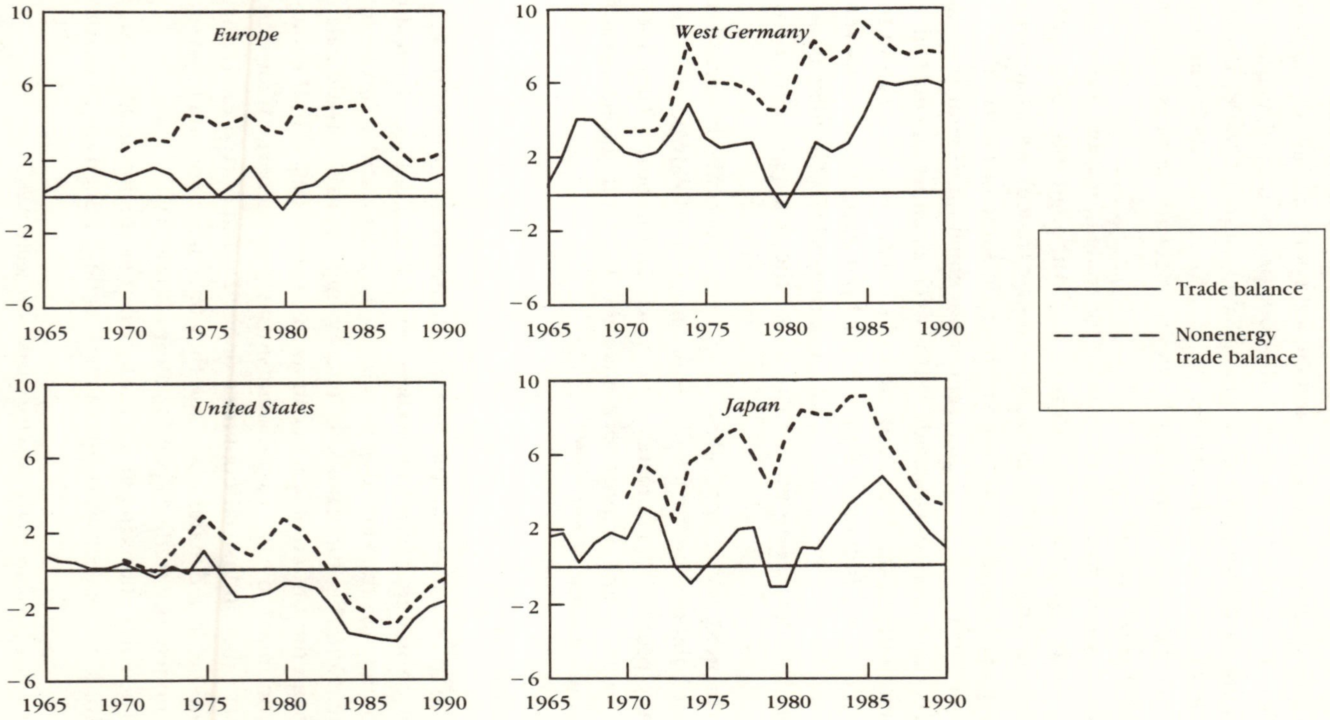

SOURCE: Organization for Economic Cooperation and Development (1991c).

and investment and that portion of trade influenced by real exchange rates. Consistent with the saving-investment framework, increased oil imports altered the composition of trade, but had only a small negative impact on the overall current account balances of most industrial countries. Meanwhile, the nonenergy trade balance rose as an offset to the increased cost of oil. How was this accomplished? In part, the increase in nonenergy exports occurred automatically, without the need for major changes in relative prices, as the oil-exporting countries increased their imports from the industrial countries. Still, imports of the Organization of Petroleum Exporting Countries (OPEC) were only about 50 percent of their exports in years of high oil prices, and 70–80 percent in years of low prices, the rest being accumulated in financial reserves. Those reserves were recycled through financial markets and at least during the 1970s were offset by the enlarged trade deficits of the developing countries. From an empirical perspective, the nonenergy trade balance also provides a much larger variance in the data with which to explore the influence of relative prices and income growth.

A great surprise, in light of the numerous arguments that trade adjustment does not work, is that large changes have taken place in the trade balances of the United States and Japan since 1985. The nonenergy trade deficit of the United States shrank from a peak of 3.0 percent of NDP in 1987 to 0.5 percent in 1990. Furthermore, contrary to much of the public rhetoric in the United States, the adjustment by Japan is substantially larger: the nonenergy trade surplus fell by nearly 6 percent of NDP between 1985 and 1990.

The adjustments by the United States and Japan seem inconsistent with the public perception that nothing has occurred in response to the change in real exchange rates since 1985. This is particularly true for Japan because of popular allegations that the net trade balance is immune to exchange rate changes: imports are constrained by nonprice factors, and the goals for exports are set without regard for cost considerations. In part, the Japanese adjustment was camouflaged by a coincident decline in world oil prices. The Japanese deficit in energy trade shrank from 5 percent of NDP in 1985 to 2 percent in 1990, negating about half of the adjustment in nonenergy trade.

In contrast, there was little adjustment in the German current account or nonenergy trade surplus before unification with East Germany. Evidence of expenditure-switching effects is not abundant because there was only a modest real appreciation of the German mark on a trade-weighted basis (see chapter 4). That change is far less than for the United States or Japan. Instead, the change since 1985 can be seen in the extent to which the German surplus has been absorbed within Europe as a whole. On a consolidated basis, the decline in the non-energy trade surplus of Europe is comparable in magnitude to the changes for the United States and Japan. As with the case of Japan, much of the adjustment has been obscured by the decline in the cost of imported oil.

Exports

One of the most striking features of an international comparison of export performance is the extent to which countries vary in the rate of export growth. Column one of table 5-1 reports the growth of non-energy exports over the period 1970–90 for the fourteen countries used in this analysis. Adjusted for inflation the volume of Japanese exports rose by 342 percent, compared with 202 percent for the United States and values ranging from 43 to 221 percent for Europe.[15] Standard explanations would trace this divergent performance either to differential rates of demand growth in their export markets or to sharply different trends in relative export prices.

Measures of growth in each country's markets for its exports were constructed by using the United Nations trade matrix to develop trade-weighted measures of GDP and imports of each nation's trading partners. Those weights are averages of the composition of each country's exports in 1977, 1980, and 1987. The UN trade weights do change over time, but the magnitude of change is not large enough to have an appreciable effect on the calculation of an index of growth in the total market. Separate weights are used for each of the twenty-two OECD countries, and other countries are first aggregated to the level of five regions.[16] The data on GDP and imports of those countries in constant prices were obtained from the OECD.

A summary measure of the growth in each country's export markets, as measured by the change in these indexes over the period 1970–90,

15. The extremes for the United Kingdom and Norway are due to the growing importance of oil in their overall exports.
16. Those regions were Africa, the Asian new industrialized economies, other Asian countries, Latin America, and OPEC. The volume indexes of GDP and imports were constructed from information obtained from the OECD Economic Outlook diskettes and the IFS data tape of the International Monetary Fund.

TABLE 5-1. *Percentage Growth in Exports and Export Markets, Constant Prices, 1970–90*

		Foreign market		Income elasticity	
	Exports[a]	GDP[b]	Imports[c]	Version (1)[d]	Version (2)[e]
		Nonenergy exports			
United States	201.8	109.2	235.1	1.85	0.86
Canada	206.5	78.1	172.0	2.65	1.20
Japan	342.3	114.6	206.2	2.99	1.66
Australia	124.5	115.2	246.9	1.08	0.50
Large European countries					
France	196.4	81.4	192.3	2.41	1.02
Germany	186.5	81.0	195.5	2.30	0.95
United Kingdom	102.4	91.2	193.1	1.12	0.53
Italy	208.6	83.0	202.8	2.51	1.03
Small European countries					
Austria	220.7	73.0	194.9	3.02	1.13
Belgium	162.8	74.2	202.1	2.19	0.80
Denmark	148.5	76.0	176.4	1.95	0.84
Netherlands	196.1	75.9	210.9	2.58	0.93
Norway	42.7	71.2	172.9	0.60	0.25
Sweden	115.7	82.2	177.4	1.41	0.65
		Manufacturing exports[f]			
United States	188.0	109.2	230.8	1.72	0.81
Canada	226.7	78.1	246.1	2.90	0.92
Japan	321.6	114.6	245.0	2.81	1.31
Australia	386.5	115.2	306.0	3.35	1.26
Large European countries					
France	194.6	81.4	219.7	2.39	0.89
Germany	166.0	81.0	222.3	2.05	0.75
United Kingdom	130.3	91.2	215.4	1.43	0.61
Italy	188.9	83.0	244.9	2.28	0.77
Small European countries					
Austria	299.5	73.0	242.0	4.10	1.24
Belgium	102.5	74.2	248.4	1.38	0.41
Denmark	194.1	76.0	225.8	2.56	0.86
Netherlands	234.2	75.9	245.5	3.09	0.95
Norway	92.7	71.2	224.3	1.30	0.41
Sweden	122.4	82.2	213.6	1.49	0.57

SOURCES: Organization for Economic Cooperation and Development (1991b and 1991c) and author's calculations as explained in the text.
a. The percentage growth of exports from 1970 to 1990.
b. Percentage growth of the trade-weighted index of GDP.
c. Percentage growth of the trade-weighted index of nonenergy imports.
d. Percentage growth in exports divided by the percentage growth in GNP.
e. Percentage growth in exports divided by the percentage growth in imports.
f. Exports and trade-weighted imports are based on manufactured products only.

is shown in columns two and three of table 5-1. Most notable in this case is the limited variation in market growth; the growth of GDP in export markets varies from a low of 71 percent for the European countries to 109 percent for the United States and 115 percent for Japan. The growth in the trade-weighted indexes of imports is substantially higher than for the GDP measure because of the faster growth of international trade, but the differences among countries are still only loosely related to the differences in export growth. In fact, imports into countries important for U.S. exports actually grew more rapidly than those of Japan, 235 percent as against 206 percent. The limited variation in long-run market growth among the countries implies that the diversity in export performance must be the result of changes in market shares, not in the differential growth of markets.[17]

Two measures of each country's trade performance are computed by dividing the growth in its exports by the corresponding trade-weighted growth of GDP and the imports of its trading partners over the period 1970–90. These ratios are shown in columns four and five of table 5-1. The ratios can also be interpreted as simple estimates of the income elasticity of each country's exports on the assumption that there was no long-run change in the relative price of exports, the real exchange rate. The implicit income elasticities for GDP are generally well above unity, with a high of 2 for Austria and Japan. At the same time, the comparison of exports with the growth of trade-weighted imports yields ratios of unity or less for many countries, again with the notable exception of Japan. On this basis the United States has suffered a loss of about 15 percent of its market share over the last 20 years. The wide variations in the growth of each country's exports in relation to growth in the trade-weighted GDP or trade-weighted imports suggest that statistical estimates of income elasticities will also vary widely across this sample of countries unless there have been compensatory changes in the relative price of their exports.

Similar calculations for manufacturing trade alone are also shown in table 5-1. At the global level manufacturing trade has grown more rapidly than total nonenergy trade, but the experience of the individual industrialized countries included in this sample is more variable. Ex-

---

17. This methodology does not adjust for differential rates of growth among product markets. Thus, it is possible that the exports of a country such as Japan grew rapidly because the product markets in which its exports are concentrated grew faster than total nonenergy imports. It was not possible to obtain data on global trade by product market as a test of this explanation.

ports of manufactures by countries such as the United States, Japan, and Germany have actually expanded at a slower rate than those of non-manufactures. The industrialized countries as a whole have suffered a loss of market share because of a faster growth of manufacturing exports from the Asian economies.

The index of trade-weighted imports as a measure of scale changes in the market for each country's exports offers some significant advantages over the index based on GDP. It yields a similar pattern of differences across countries, but it simplifies some of the problems of dealing with lags in the response of trade to changes in income. In the regression analysis the import index is more closely correlated with year-to-year changes in each country's exports. Indexes of foreign demand that incorporate the trade patterns of each country's exports performed better than a single index of global trade, although the indexes for the European countries were highly correlated with one another. For example, the impact on the United States of the sharp reversal of economic growth in Latin America during the 1980s is clearly evident in the trade-weighted indexes. The use of the index of trade-weighted imports also simplifies the regression analysis by eliminating the need to include a measure of reductions in national barriers to imports. It is the scale variable in all of the reported regression results.[18]

A substantial number of alternative measures of relative prices have been used in past empirical studies of trade flows. The analysis of exchange rate movements in chapter 4 reported on the relative performance of measures based on a comparison of GDP price deflators, consumer price indexes, unit labor costs in manufacturing, producer prices of manufactures, and export prices.[19] The results from that analysis favored the use of producer prices, as in the Morgan Guaranty measures of the real exchange rate, or relative export prices. Similar results were obtained in some preliminary experiments using different measures of the relative price of domestic and foreign-produced goods

18. The use of total imports might appear to lead to an underestimate of the price elasticities because it eliminates the effects of price competition between the exporting country and the domestic production of the importing country. As long as the exporter accounts for a small share of imports into any one country, this is likely to be a minor problem because the imports are weighted over so many countries. In any case, the alternative of a traded-weighted index of GDP has no uniform tendency to increase the estimated price elasticities.

19. Each index was constructed as the ratio of the domestic price to a trade-weighted foreign price, where the latter was converted to the domestic currency equivalent using nominal exchange rates. The country weights were those employed in the Morgan Guaranty exchange rate indexes.

to explain the trade flows. The real exchange rate indexes of Morgan Guaranty and relative export prices provided the strongest correlations. Presumably the reason for the improved performance is that these indexes exclude a larger portion of nontraded goods in the construction of the price indexes. For some countries, Japan being the most extreme example, this distinction is very important because the prices of tradable goods—basically, manufactures—has increased much less than those of nontradables. Unit labor costs, for example, do not appear to provide an accurate measure of trade competitiveness because large cyclical fluctuations limit their reliability as an indicator of changes in marginal costs.

There are two significant problems with relying on measures of export prices to estimate the trade elasticities. First, the export price index is used to deflate data on trade flows in nominal terms in order to obtain the series on the volume of exports. If the same index is included as a component of the relative price of exports in a regression, the estimates of the price elasticity may be greatly biased. Second, a price index that covers only those goods actually traded may fail to indicate the full extent of any price disadvantage or advantage if the producers of those products set their prices so as to meet the competition in the global market. Instead, cost differences would be absorbed by variations in the profit rate on exports. These problems are minimized by relying on a broader measure of domestic prices, which is constructed independently of the price deflator for exports and is more likely to reflect domestic cost pressures. The use of nonfood, nonfuel manufactured goods prices, as in the Morgan Guaranty index, seems to be a reasonable compromise. It is not so broad as to be dominated by nontradables; yet it includes the prices of goods sold in the domestic market, as well as abroad. The reported equations are based on the Morgan Guaranty indexes unless the improvement in the statistical fit using the export price was large and not associated with a larger price coefficient for the first period, where the potential for statistical bias is most severe.

Many previous empirical studies of trade have separated the issue of what determines import and export prices from the estimation of the response of trade flows to those prices. This allows them to deal explicitly with the question of pricing-to-market and the lags in the adjustment of trade prices to changes in domestic and foreign prices. The formulation used in this analysis embeds the lags in the adjustment of export prices into the overall lag structure by relying primarily on economy-wide price indexes to compute the measure of the real exchange rate.

TABLE 5-2. *Regression Equations for Nonenergy Exports, Logarithms, 1970–90*

Country	Global imports	Relative price[a]	Time trend	R^2	Standard error	Durbin-Watson
United States	0.17	−1.02	3.35	0.991	0.031	1.4
	(1.3)	(8.9)	(4.5)			
Canada	0.23	−0.96	4.19	0.989	0.045	1.4
	(1.8)	(3.7)	(5.5)			
Japan	1.57	−0.51	−1.41	0.995	0.036	1.4
	(7.9)	(4.1)	(1.2)			
Australia	0.20	−0.66	2.06	0.948	0.060	0.7
	(0.7)	(2.9)	(1.1)			
Large European countries						
France	1.11	−1.18	−0.75	0.998	0.012	2.2
	(13.3)	(4.6)	(2.0)			
Germany	0.67	−0.29	1.31	0.992	0.030	1.1
	(3.0)	(1.0)	(1.2)			
United Kingdom	0.27	−0.59	2.43	0.982	0.028	1.1
	(2.2)	(7.7)	(3.6)			
Italy	0.70	−0.76	1.48	0.993	0.031	1.6
	(3.7)	(2.4)	(1.6)			
Small European countries						
Austria	0.92	−0.63	1.66	0.995	0.027	0.7
	(5.9)	(1.4)	(2.1)			
Belgium	1.39	−1.48	−2.77	0.995	0.019	1.3
	(8.4)	(5.0)	(3.4)			
Denmark	0.68	−1.04	1.13	0.996	0.016	2.0
	(4.0)	(6.0)	(1.5)			
Netherlands	0.91	−0.33	0.56	0.994	0.027	0.9
	(4.8)	(1.5)	(0.7)			
Sweden	0.46	−0.92	0.98	0.983	0.035	1.0
	(2.0)	(3.7)	(0.8)			

SOURCE: Author's calculations as explained in the text. T-statistics are in parentheses. Nonenergy exports and global imports are measured in constant prices.

a. Relative wholesale prices, except for Belgium, Denmark, and France, where relative export prices are used.

A set of preliminary regressions for nonenergy exports is shown in table 5-2. In logarithms, nonenergy exports are regressed on the index of trade-weighted imports of trading partners, the real exchange rate with lags extending over three years, and a simple trend term.[20] The

20. The lag between the change in foreign income and imports is captured by the use of the trade-weighted foreign imports as the scale variable. There was no evidence of any further lag between changes in foreign imports and each country's exports.

trend term is included because without it the regressions are forced to allocate the growth of exports either to the growth of income or to the change in the real exchange rate. By eliminating the possibility of any other influences on exports the regression may misstate the extent of correlation between exports and the two independent variables. If a trend term is included, the contributions of growth in the market and relative prices are estimated in terms of the deviations from their trends; this exercise is close to estimating of the relationship in first differences.[21] On the other hand, the index of trade-weighted imports is highly correlated with the trend.

The estimated price elasticities generally have high statistical significance, but they vary greatly in magnitude among the countries in the sample. There is even greater variation in the magnitude of the coefficient on the scale variable, which is intended to measure the growth in the market for each country's exports. The coefficients are significantly below the value of unity, which would be consistent with a constant market share for the United States, Canada, Australia, the United Kingdom, and Sweden.

Similar regressions, shown in appendix table 5A-1, were estimated for manufacturing exports. Disaggregation down to the level of manufactures makes little difference. The coefficients on relative prices are normally significant and show a similar pattern with respect to which countries had the largest price elasticities. Although the income coefficients continue to vary substantially, there is a greater tendency for their values to cluster around unity.

These results suggest a slight modification of the estimated equation to constrain the scale coefficient to unity. The trend term can then be more readily interpreted as reflecting the residual portion of the change in market share that cannot be accounted for by the variation in relative prices. The results for the constrained estimation are shown in table 5-3. The assumption of a unitary scale elasticity is strongly rejected only for the United States, Canada, and the United Kingdom. The exports of these countries continue to show a low sensitivity to variations in foreign demand with a large positive time trend. The constraint has little effect on the estimates of the price elasticities, which are generally

---

21. The sign of the coefficient on the trend term is of interest in its own right in view of the discussion of a secular decline in some countries' competitiveness, as measured by factors other than relative prices alone. See, for example, Krugman and Baldwin (1987).

TABLE 5-3. *Constrained Regression Equations for Nonenergy Exports,*
Logarithms, 1970–90

Country	Global imports	Relative price[a]	Time trend	Standard error	Durbin-Watson	ρ
United States	0.17	−1.02	3.35	0.031	1.5	c
	(1.3)	(8.9)	(4.5)			
Canada	0.23	−0.96	4.18	0.045	1.4	c
	(1.8)	(3.7)	(5.5)			
Japan	1.0	−0.50	1.81	0.043	1.1	c
		(3.4)	(9.7)			
Australia	1.0	−0.85	−2.64	0.070	1.0	c
		(3.3)	(8.8)			
Large European countries						
France	1.0	−0.97	−0.25	0.013	1.9	c
		(4.4)	(4.2)			
Germany	1.0	−0.62	−0.21	0.027	1.3	0.6
		(2.2)	(1.0)			
United Kingdom	0.27	−0.59	2.43	0.028	1.1	c
	(2.2)	(7.7)	(3.6)			
Italy	1.0	−0.38	b	0.032	1.7	c
		(1.9)				
Small European countries						
Austria	1.0	−0.90	1.58	0.021	1.9	0.6
		(2.0)	(2.7)			
Belgium	1.0	−1.01	−0.85	0.022	1.5	c
		(4.0)	(9.3)			
Denmark	1.0	−1.23	−0.34	0.018	2.4	c
		(8.0)	(4.2)			
Netherlands	1.0	−0.31	b	0.021	1.4	0.7
		(2.0)				
Sweden	1.0	−1.22	−1.65	0.023	1.2	0.8
		(4.8)	(5.4)			

SOURCE: Author's calculations as explained in text. T-statistics are in parentheses. Nonenergy exports and global imports are measured in constant prices.
a. Relative wholesale prices, except for Belgium, Denmark, and France, where relative export prices are used.
b. Variable excluded from regression.
c. No significant autocorrelation.

near unity, but it simplifies the identification of those countries for whom exports have exceeded or fallen short of growth in their export markets. For the United States the low correlation between exports and growth in its markets seems to be solely a reflection of the more diverse nature of its exports because the same problem is much less evident for manufacturing exports, as shown in appendix table 5A-2. The low scale elasticities for Canada and the United Kingdom, however, were also evident for their exports of manufactures.

The frequency with which the trend coefficients are statistically significant implies that factors other than exchange rates have important effects in a country's share of its export markets. The elimination of the trend generally reduces, rather than increases, the significance of the real exchange rate. Perhaps the explanation lies in the product composition of exports; but, if so, it is at a level of disaggregation greater than for manufacturing because the trend is equally important for the manufacturing export equations. This issue is not explored here because of the lack of data on imports by country and product line. There was also evidence of significant auto-correlation in the residuals for four countries.

A test was also made to explore the possibility that supply constraints in the exporting country result in an underestimate of the sensitivity of exports to foreign demand and relative prices. This was done by including the level of potential output, as measured by the OECD, or the ratio of GDP to potential output, in the export equations. Because these variables were significant in very few countries with variable signs, there appears to be no uniform evidence of capacity effects. Nor did the magnitude of the price elasticities appear to increase when the capacity terms were included.

The index of trade-weighted imports provides a more precise measure than an index of foreign GDPs of the effect of changes in foreign economic activity on country's exports. However, it leaves incomplete the determination of the response of imports to changes in domestic demand conditions. The relationship between imports and domestic demand changes is explored more fully in the following section, but for the present it can be described in a simple way by a regression in logarithms of the index of trade-weighted imports on the level of the index of trade-weighted GDP, its change over the prior period, and a trend term. The regression coefficients were very similar for all of the countries. A representative example is provided by the results for the United States:

$$WM = 1.15 * WGDP + 2.52 * (WGDP - WGDP_{-1}) +$$

(5-3) $\quad$ (6.2) $\qquad\qquad$ (3.5)

$$1.86 * T,$$

$\qquad$ (2.8)

where *WM* = the trade-weighted index of imports,
     WGDP = the trade-weighted index of GDP, and
     T = a simple trend.

The long-run elasticity with respect to GDP is close to unity for all the countries while the coefficient on short-run cyclical changes in demand is normally large and positive. This result is consistent with an interpretation of the global market as a residual source of supply that bears the brunt of short-run variations in domestic demand. Furthermore, the coefficient on the time trend was uniformly positive, as expected during a period of liberalization of international trade.

In summary, it is possible to account for a large proportion of the variation in exports of the industrial countries by means of simple regressions that emphasize changes in foreign demand and real exchange rates. The estimates of the price elasticities are nearly always statistically significant; but, with long-run elasticities in the range of 0.5 to 1.0, they fall far short of implying that domestic and foreign-produced goods are perfect substitutes. Estimates of the response to changes in foreign demand are more variable. The significance of the trend terms, however, suggests that it may be misleading to assume that differences in the secular growth of a country's exports reflect differences in income elasticities.

Imports

Somewhat surprisingly, there are greater problems in estimating the income and price elasticities for imports than for exports. In particular, the choice of a specific index to represent variations in domestic economic activity has substantial implications for the estimates of the price elasticity. An initial set of estimates is shown in table 5-4. The activity variable is GDP and the estimated price elasticity is based on a three-year polynomial lag of the Morgan Guaranty real exchange rate. The income elasticities of imports are generally above 2.0.[22] As mentioned in the discussion of exports, the high income elasticity merely follows from the fact that the growth of imports has exceeded that of income. With no other scale variable in the regression, the income elasticity must exceed 1 simply to match the trends in the data. When a simple

22. Lawrence (1990) obtained even larger income elasticities—about 2.5—for the United States.

TABLE 5-4. *Regression Equations for Nonenergy Imports, GDP as Demand Measure, Logarithms, 1970–90*

Country	Gross domestic product	Relative price	R^2	Standard error	Durbin-Watson
United States	2.14	0.89	0.987	0.046	0.9
	(35.2)	(7.9)			
Canada	2.12	0.03	0.996	0.031	1.7
	(38.4)	(0.2)			
Japan	1.33	1.38	0.960	0.089	1.2
	(13.7)	(4.4)			
Australia	1.85	0.43	0.979	0.052	2.2
	(24.7)	(2.3)			
Large European countries					
France	2.27	0.59	0.992	0.032	1.3
	(38.3)	(3.0)			
Germany	2.36	−0.31	0.994	0.026	1.9
	(52.6)	(1.7)			
United Kingdom	2.40	0.28	0.991	0.036	0.9
	(29.7)	(3.4)			
Italy	1.94	1.77	0.985	0.045	1.0
	(29.1)	(5.8)			
Small European countries					
Austria	2.07	0.44	0.996	0.025	1.4
	(13.1)	(1.4)			
Belgium	2.96	0.55	0.988	0.039	1.8
	(21.4)	(4.5)			
Denmark	1.68	0.19	0.984	0.031	2.0
	(30.6)	(1.3)			
Netherlands	2.33	−0.41	0.990	0.030	1.8
	(25.7)	(2.3)			
Sweden	2.14	0.75	0.986	0.030	2.2
	(23.1)	(3.6)			

SOURCES: Author's calculations as explained in the text and GDP measured in constant prices. T-statistics are in parentheses.

time trend was added in a second set of regressions, however, the magnitude of the income elasticity often increased, while the coefficient on the trend was negative. The income elasticity for Japan, for example, rose to 4.2, with a large negative trend coefficient. Furthermore, efforts to attribute the high income elasticity to cyclical effects—by including capacity utilization or the change in GDP—seldom resulted in significant coefficients and did not reduce the estimate of the long-run elasticity. At the same time, the coefficients on the real exchange rate are highly variable across countries and statistically insignificant in several cases.

Although consistent with prior studies, the finding of a high income elasticity seems questionable. It attributes nearly all of the growth in the share of imports in GDP to a general expansion of incomes, leaving little or no role for trade liberalization.[23] Furthermore, the results are quite different from the conclusions about the behavior of the trade-weighted imports, as reported at the end of the discussion of exports. In that analysis the long-run income elasticity was near unity with a high short-run effect of income change, and there was evidence of secular growth in imports independent of the expansion of GDP.

One possible explanation is that GDP, which includes both tradables and nontradables, systematically understates the variation in demand for the market basket of tradables of which imports is a component. Since the tradables sector is composed largely of goods, it is far more variable than GNP over the business cycle, even though the two have similar long-term trends. In the regressions a large coefficient on GDP is required to generate the short-run variability in tradables. At the same time, a large coefficient is consistent with the fact that imports have also grown more rapidly than GDP in the long run.

As an alternative, industrial production is substituted for GDP in the import demand equations. The two measures differ primarily in that the index of industrial production excludes the output of the services sectors which have low cyclical variability. For the countries in the sample the variance of annual changes in industrial production is two to three times larger than that for GDP. Yet, industrial production is not growing more rapidly than GDP; in fact, between 1970 and 1990 the industrial sector of most countries grew slightly less than GDP.

The choice of a specific measure of relative prices for imports raised many of the same issues as were previously discussed for the export equations. A measure of the relative price of domestic versus foreign-produced products based on producer prices, the Morgan Guaranty real exchange rate index, produces smaller errors and more significant coefficients than indexes based on a comparison of GDP, consumer prices, or unit labor costs. However, an additional measure was com-

---

23. Since the alternative measures of the real exchange rate, discussed in chapter 4, revealed little apparent trend, the impact of trade liberalization operating through relative prices cannot be very important in the estimated regressions.

puted as the ratio of the domestic producer price to the import price deflator, bypassing any use of the nominal exchange rate index to compute local currency equivalents of the foreign price indexes. The two relative price measures have the same numerator, domestic wholesale prices, but they differ in the measure of the foreign price in the denominator. For the Morgan Guaranty (MG) index the denominator is the foreign producer price times the exchange rate. For the alternative measure it is the price deflator for nonenergy imports.[24]

A representative set of revised import volume equations, in which industrial production is the activity variable, is shown in table 5-5. With industrial production substituted for GDP, the income elasticities are much lower. If the standard error of the equations alone is taken into account, however, there is little to choose between the two measures of economic activity. The difference lies in the positive trend term for the version using industrial production and the increased statistical significance of the relative price term in equations that use industrial production. A parallel set of equations for manufacturing imports is shown in table 5A-3.

The choice between the two alternative measures of relative prices was governed by whichever index yielded the smallest residual error for the overall equation. More frequently than was the case with exports, the import price deflator is preferred (six countries).[25] It makes a substantial difference in the estimates of the price elasticities for Canada, Germany, and the United Kingdom. For some other countries the improvement only amounts to smaller residual errors.

Both forms of the equation were acceptable for the United States in terms of highly significant coefficients on both the income and price variables. The use of the MG real exchange rate yields a price elasticity of 1.1, compared with 1.4 in the version using import prices reported in table 5-5, and a standard error of estimates of 0.05 compared to 0.03 for the equation shown in the table. The measure of relative prices based on the import price deflator has a narrower range of variation,

---

24. For the United States the trend in the import price index is similar to that in the foreign price, with a substantial dampening of the fluctuations. This result is consistent with the argument that importers adjust their prices to meet competition in the domestic market. For several other countries, however, the two indexes simply look very different over parts of the data period.

25. In order to ensure that the improvement was not due to measurement errors, the equations were also estimated with an instrumental variable representation of the import price deflator. In those cases where the import price deflator was used, the instrumented equation yielded similar coefficients.

TABLE 5-5. *Regression Equations for Nonenergy Imports, Industrial Production as Activity Variable, Logarithms, 1970–90*

Country	Industrial production	Relative price	Time trend	R^2	Standard error	Durbin-Watson	ρ
United States[a]	0.97	1.43	0.037	0.99	0.03	1.9	[c]
	(5.8)	(12.4)	(7.4)				
Canada[a]	1.07	0.60	0.031	0.99	0.03	1.7	0.5
	(5.4)	(1.3)	(2.0)				
Japan	1.60	0.97	[b]	0.98	0.07	1.6	0.7
	(10.1)	(2.8)					
Australia	1.68	0.63	0.030	0.98	0.05	2.0	[c]
	(3.3)	(2.9)	(4.0)				
Large European countries							
France[a]	1.42	0.80	0.030	0.99	0.01	2.4	[c]
	(14.1)	(9.9)	(19.7)				
Germany[a]	0.90	1.41	0.027	0.99	0.03	1.4	0.6
	(3.9)	(2.1)	(3.9)				
United Kingdom[a]	0.73	0.33	0.041	0.99	0.02	1.7	[c]
	(9.8)	(2.7)	(11.1)				
Italy	1.40	1.53	0.025	0.99	0.03	1.3	[c]
	(8.5)	(7.0)	(7.0)				
Small European countries							
Austria	1.37	0.89	0.008	0.99	0.03	1.4	[c]
	(8.2)	(2.2)	(1.1)				
Belgium[a]	1.23	0.99	0.040	0.99	0.03	1.8	[c]
	(5.9)	(8.4)	(0.04)				
Denmark[a]	1.15	0.32	[b]	0.99	0.03	2.1	[c]
	(24.7)	(2.1)					
Netherlands	1.23	0.61	0.012	0.99	0.03	1.7	[c]
	(6.1)	(4.2)	(2.7)				
Sweden	1.08	1.01	0.032	0.99	0.03	2.8	[c]
	(5.7)	(5.6)	(16.4)				

SOURCES: Author's calculations as explained in the text. T-statistics are in parentheses. Nonenergy imports and industrial production are measured in constant prices.
a. Relative price is based on the ratio of the domestic wholesale price to the import price deflator.
b. Variable excluded from regression.
c. No significant autocorrelation.

and thus a larger coefficient. An important distinction arises in the 1988-89 period when the version based on the MG index underpredicts the volume of imports by a substantial margin.

The estimated price elasticities are generally larger and more significant than those of table 5-4. Just as for exports, however, the variation in the magnitude of the price elasticities is difficult to explain. There is no clear reason as to why some countries have high reported price elasticities and others low ones. Yet those differences remain for a variety of specifications. The estimated price elasticity was consistently high for the United States, Japan, Italy, and Sweden, whereas it was particularly low for the United Kingdom and Denmark.

Divergent Income Elasticities: A Digression

The calculations described in this chapter indicate that income elasticities for both exports and imports differ substantially among the countries under investigation. The differences were most pronounced on the export side, and they were evident for a wide range of formulations, even though the income elasticities were treated as fixed parameters throughout. As discussed in the introduction, Krugman has suggested that the income elasticities may, in fact, be endogenous in the sense that they are systematically related to a country's rate of economic growth. This is an important point because it implies that a deterioration in a country's trade balance is far less likely to be a constraint on its growth rate than is commonly assumed.

As a partial test of Krugman's hypothesis, data from the fourteen countries were used to estimate pooled regressions for both exports and imports in which the income elasticities were made a function of the rate of growth of GDP. This was done by estimating a regression in logarithms of the form

$$(5\text{-}4) \qquad Y_i = \alpha_i + (\beta_i + \gamma G_i) * GDP_i + \tau REX_i$$

$$i = 1,14,$$

where Y_i = either exports or imports, GDP_i = domestic GDP for imports and the trade-weighted index of foreign GDP for exports, REX_i = a three-year average of the Morgan Guaranty real exchange rate, and G = a ten-year average of the country's past growth rate for GDP.

In this formulation, the income elasticity is allowed to vary across countries by including specific country dummies; but it also changes over time in response to changes in each country's long-term rate of economic growth. The coefficient on the growth rate and the real exchange rate are constrained to be the same for all countries. Because the β_i coefficient is allowed to vary with each country, only changes in growth rates over time, not differences among countries, are used to estimate the value of the coefficient, γ. The pooled formulation was required because there is insufficient variation in individual countries over only twenty years of data to provide useful results. The values of γ obtained from the regressions were 0.067 ($t = 5.9$) for exports and 0.11 ($t = 5.2$) for imports. By allowing for a variable coefficient on the activity variable, it was possible to obtain slightly larger estimates of the price elasticities in the pooled regressions.[26]

The results provide support for the basic notion that income elasticities may be endogenously determined. They do not, however, indicate that an endogenous adjustment of the elasticities prevents the emergence of trade deficits during a period of high growth. Support for Krugman's hypothesis requires a positive influence of growth on the income elasticity of exports, and a negative coefficient for imports. Instead, the income coefficients for both imports and exports vary positively with past growth rates. The magnitude and significance of these coefficients, together with the instability of these parameters in the earlier analysis, suggest that Krugman has raised an important question about the validity of empirical models that assume a fixed income elasticity for trade flows, even if his explanation may be incomplete.

Nonenergy Trade Balances

The export and import equations can be used to estimate the effects of changes in relative prices and incomes on the overall trade balance in volume terms. However, additional equations explaining the behavior of import and export prices would be required to obtain estimates of the effect on the nominal trade balance. An alternative method is to estimate a reduced form of the nominal trade balance that embeds the determination of import and export prices into the estimation of the overall coefficient on the real exchange rate. This approach makes it unnecessary to rely on the import and export price deflators, whose quality is suspect; and it provides an additional check on the reasonableness of the coefficients obtained from the two volume equations. It also yields a direct summary measure of the effectiveness of exchange rates in altering net trade flows.

The main disadvantage is that the collinearity between the measures of domestic and foreign economic activity make it difficult to estimate

---

26. Equations that used the alternative measures of the activity variable or a single fixed value for β yielded similar results.

the income elasticities. As mentioned earlier, the estimated income elasticities are already of limited reliability in the individual export and import equations, and one merely compounds that problem by focusing on the trade balance. The approach adopted here is to constrain the income or scale elasticities to the values implied by the underlying export and import equations, and to use the estimation of the trade balance equations to focus on the effect of changes in the real exchange rate.[27]

The equations for the net trade balance are reported in table 5-6. The dependent variable is the logarithm of the ratio of nominal exports to nonenergy imports. In general, the equations incorporate the constraint that the absolute value of the scale coefficients on trade-weighted imports and domestic industrial production are both equal to unity. Exceptions were made for those countries for which the original export and import equations rejected the assumption of unity at the 95 percent confidence level. This left only the relative price and the trend coefficient to be estimated statistically.

The results are by and large more encouraging with respect to the effectiveness of changes in real exchange rates in reallocating trade flows than is implied by the price elasticities for exports and imports individually. The relative price coefficients for the net nominal trade balance should equal unity plus the coefficient from the export equation minus the price coefficient of the import equation.[28] A negative coefficient indicates that real devaluation is an effective means of improving the trade balance. The results are strongly suggestive of a large effect of relative prices on the trade balance. In most cases the price elasticity in the trade balance equation is larger than the value obtained from the two trade volume equations (the exceptions being the United States, Canada, Germany, and Belgium). The two countries for which the sum of the coefficients previously fell short of unity, the United Kingdom and the Netherlands, have price coefficients in the nominal-balance equations well below zero. In all cases the absolute magnitude

---

27. A further disadvantage is that the extent of any pricing to market on the import side is assumed to be matched by similar behavior on the export side. Otherwise, we cannot continue to impose the constraint, implied by the use of a relative price variable, that the coefficient on the foreign price index is equal and opposite in sign to that on the domestic price.

28. The addition of unity results from the conversion to nominal values. The condition would not be expected to hold precisely because different measures of the relative price were used in some of the volume equations.

TABLE 5-6. *Regression Equations for Nominal Nonenergy Trade Balance Logarithms, 1970–90*[a]

Country	Global imports	Industrial production	Relative prices	Time trend	Standard error	Durbin-Watson
United States	1.0	−1.0	−1.01 (10.5)	−0.048 (36.2)	0.036	1.5
Canada	0.35	−1.0	−0.44 (4.5)	−0.091 (3.5)	0.025	1.6
Japan	1.0	−1.6	−1.59 (6.6)	0.019 (7.2)	0.060	2.0
Australia	1.0	−1.0	−1.07 (2.8)	−0.058 (10.7)	0.072	1.5
Large European countries						
France	1.0	−1.0	−1.00 (4.1)	−0.042 (23.5)	0.035	1.7
Germany	1.0	−1.0	−0.62 (2.2)	−0.029 (14.9)	0.043	1.0
United Kingdom	0.5	−0.8	−0.88 (6.7)	−0.022 (10.2)	0.029	1.9
Italy	1.0	−1.4	−1.24 (4.1)	−0.022 (10.6)	0.043	1.6
Small European countries						
Austria	1.0	−1.0	−1.64 (2.7)	[b]	0.036	1.2
Belgium	1.0	−1.0	−0.88 (9.0)	−0.055 (22.6)	0.020	2.5
Denmark	1.0	−1.0	−0.70 (3.0)	−0.007 (4.4)	0.048	1.6
Netherlands	1.0	−1.0	−1.11 (7.5)	−0.017 (10.9)	0.028	1.2
Norway	1.0	−1.0	−1.70 (2.1)	−0.043 (7.3)	0.071	1.2
Sweden	1.0	−1.0	−2.11 (5.4)	−0.053 (17.1)	0.046	1.7

SOURCES: Author's calculations as explained in the text. T-statistics are in parentheses. Global imports and industrial production are measured in constant prices.

a. The real exchange rate is based on wholesale prices except for Australia, Canada, Germany, and the United Kingdom, where export prices are used.

b. Variable excluded from regression.

of the relative price coefficient is substantial and of high statistical significance.

The source of the larger estimated price elasticities is somewhat uncertain. Differences are expected, in part because there was some variation in the measure of relative prices that was used in the individual export and import equations, and in part because the trade balance regressions rely more heavily on the Morgan Guaranty index of the real exchange rate. In regressions using a measure of the trade balance in volume terms, the estimated price elasticities departed only slightly from the those implied by the individual export and import equations. Furthermore, the residuals from the export and import volume equations were not significantly correlated with one another for any of the countries in the sample. The largest change occurred in the shift from the formulation of the relationship in physical volume terms to a direct estimation of the nominal trade balance. This result is most consistent with the argument that the import and export price deflators are measured with some error, and that those errors cause the volume equations to underestimate the influence of changes in relative prices.

An interesting finding in table 5-6 is the negative coefficient on the trend term for all the countries in the sample except Japan and Austria. A negative trend implies a need to accept a steady decline in the real exchange rates, and perhaps the terms of trade, to maintain any given trade balance. This is not a new finding for the United States.[29] The surprise is that the coefficient is negative for so many countries. In fact, the size of the coefficient for the United States is not out of line with that of several other industrial countries. This result is obviously very sensitive to the relative magnitude of the two scale coefficients; and, as mentioned previously, there is considerable uncertainty about the precise way to measure the trend in the real exchange rate because it is affected by the choice of specific national price indexes required to construct it. The negative time trend appears to result from the increased penetration of global markets by Asian countries. These countries are not included in the calculations of the relative price index.

Although tests of the stability of the trade balance equations are limited by the short span of the available data, two possibilities are to reestimate the equations excluding five years first from the beginning and then from the end of the full estimation period. Limiting the estimation period to 1970–85 had little effect. There was no particular

---

29. See, for example, Krugman and Baldwin (1985).

tendency for the price coefficients to either rise or fall; and the estimates were within 20 percent of those for the full period for eleven of
the fourteen countries. The greatest instability appeared in the results
for Australia, France, and the United Kingdom. In the 1975–90 period
there was a greater tendency for the price elasticities to increase in
relation to the full period; but for eight countries the change was less
than 10 percent. The coefficient varied by amounts in excess of 30
percent for Australia, Austria, Italy, the Netherlands, and Norway. The
fact that the estimated elasticities do not decline for the 1975–90 period seems directly counter to arguments that the response of trade
flows to changed real exchange rates after 1985 were smaller than
expected.

Another test of the equations was to examine their performance
during the periods of large changes in oil prices. The oil price increases
of 1973 and 1979 and the collapse of 1986 were severe shocks to the
international economy. For countries such as Japan, which import a
large part of their energy, the increased oil import bill implied a need
to generate large earnings from nonenergy trade.[30] As shown in figure
5-1, most energy-importing countries did build much larger surpluses
on nonenergy trade, rather than let the costs be absorbed in a reduced
overall trade balance. This inverse relationship between the oil and
non-oil trade balances can also be illustrated with a simple regression
relating the nonenergy trade balance to the balance in energy trade,
both measured as a share of GDP. With the addition of a time trend the
coefficient on the energy trade balance was invariably negative, between -0.5 and -1.0, and statistically significant.

According to the trade model presented in this chapter, the adjustment to the increased energy trade deficit would have required either
a decline in the real exchange rate or a reduced rate of income growth
and imports in relation to each country's trading partners. Thus it is
useful to ask whether the sharp changes in the energy trade balance
affected nonenergy trade through some other mechanism. As a simple
test, the equations of table 5-6 were reestimated with the addition of
each country's energy trade balance measured as a percentage of GDP.
Once allowance was made for the influence of changes in economic
activity and relative prices, there was no evidence of a significant negative correlation with the energy trade balance. On the whole, the

30. One exception would be if the oil price increase were expected to be temporary,
and individuals planned to borrow to finance the higher outlays.

TABLE 5-7. *Trade Balance as a Percent of GDP, Sensitivity to Changes in Global Imports and Relative Prices, Fourteen Countries*
Percent of GDP

	10 percent change in:		
Country	Global imports	Relative prices	1990 nonenergy trade share
United States	0.94	0.94	0.09
Canada	0.81	1.02	0.23
Japan	1.00	1.58	0.10
Australia	1.46	1.57	0.15
Large European countries			
France	2.17	2.17	0.22
Germany	2.84	1.76	0.28
United Kingdom	1.23	2.05	0.24
Italy	1.95	2.42	0.19
Small European countries			
Austria	3.91	6.41	0.39
Belgium	6.89	6.06	0.69
Denmark	3.12	2.18	0.31
Netherlands	4.93	5.48	0.49
Norway	3.33	5.66	0.33
Sweden	2.87	6.06	0.29

SOURCES: Table 5-6 and author's calculations as explained in the text.

coefficients on the energy trade balance were very small and of varying signs, and never approached statistical significance at the 0.95 level.

A final exercise was to transform the results from the estimation of the trade equations into a form more useful for thinking about the relationship between changes in trade balances and domestic saving-investment balances. In chapter 3 variations in the SI balance were expressed as a share of GDP. In table 5-7 the income and price elasticities from table 5-6 are transformed to a similar format by evaluating the change in the net trade balance (expressed as a percentage of GDP) that would result from a 10 percent change in global trade and a 10 percent change in the real exchange rate of each country. The estimates can be obtained by multiplying the price elasticities of table 5-6 by the ratio of the average of nonenergy exports and imports to GDP. The trade shares used for that calculation are shown in column three of table 5-7. The result is a substantially modified ranking of the countries in terms of the magnitude of change in the real exchange rate required to bring the trade balance in line with a given change in the domestic saving-investment balance. Although the trade elasticities were high for the United States, the low share of trade in GDP implies that a 10 percent change in the real exchange rate would alter the external balance by about 1 percent of GDP. The magnitude of change in the trade balance, expressed as a share of GDP, is far larger for the European countries where trade is more important. For these countries a 10 percent change in the exchange rate would alter the trade balance by 2 to 6 percent of GDP.

If the potential magnitude of fluctuation in the domestic saving-investment balance is the same for all countries, the required range of fluctuation in the real exchange rates is inherently larger for countries with low shares of trade in GDP. Thus it is perhaps not surprising that the European countries, with their large trade sectors, are more willing than the United States to adhere to a fixed exchange rate system.[31] Except for massive shocks, such as the unification of Germany, the realignment of trade balances to changed domestic saving-investment balances can be accomplished through tolerable variations in relative rates of domestic price inflation without having to alter the nominal exchange rate. In the case of the United States and Japan, however, the required change in relative prices is much larger. In the mid-1980s the U.S. current account deficit was about 2.5 percent of GDP. According to the estimates of table 5-7, to restore a balance, while leaving relative incomes unchanged, the domestic price level would have had to fall by 25 percent. No wonder the United States views nominal exchange rate flexibility as an essential element of the international economic system.

Conclusion

The major principle that emerges from the empirical analysis in this chapter is that exchange rate changes are an effective means of altering trade flows. The effect on the nominal trade balance of changes in the real exchange rate is large and highly significant statistically for a wide sample of industrial countries. In general, trade equations of the type used in earlier empirical studies continue to perform quite well in explaining changes in trade flows over the 1980s. The emergence of large trade imbalances during the decade do not seem inexplicable, in

31. The large trade shares are largely a reflection of trade within Europe. Thus we would reach similar conclusions for the individual states of the United States if it were possible to obtain trade data. In fact, the arguments of McKinnon and Mundell about the unimportance of the nominal exchange rate are plausible for the individual American states, given what are probably even higher trade shares and basic price elasticities.

view of the changes in real exchange rates and relative rates of income growth.

The results raise some questions about the empirical research in two areas. First, the long-run income elasticities of trade appear to be lower than previously indicated. Studies that used GDP as the measure of scale changes generally obtained income elasticities of about 2.0, whereas this study suggests that long-run income elasticities are closer to unity and that a larger portion of the growth in trade as a share of GDP should be attributed to other secular factors such as trade liberalization. The short-run results are similar to the prior study once it is recognized that industrial production, used as a proxy for the production of tradable goods, has a much larger cyclical variability than GDP. However, the estimates of income elasticities remain ambiguous because the differences among countries in the growth of trade are not fully understood. One possible explanation that could be explored concerns the wide variation in the growth of specific product markets and in the product composition of trade from country to country.

Second, the estimated price elasticities are somewhat larger than those obtained in prior studies. The higher price elasticities may be due in part to the use of producer prices, in relation to a trade-weighted average of trading partners, in the construction of the real exchange rate.

The results are also striking when viewed from the perspective of the current discussions of trade policy, particularly the debate with Japan. To begin with, the popular perception that no adjustment has taken place despite large exchange rate changes clearly seems to be wrong. The analysis does not support the argument that the actual adjustment has been less than what should have been expected on the basis of historical data. The disappointment seems to have been largely a creation of various commentators' own erroneous expectations.

Furthermore, the perception that U.S. trade is particularly insensitive to exchange rate changes or that the response to the post-1985 decline of the dollar was asymmetric to the response to its increase in 1981–85 is not supported by the data. The price elasticity estimates are more stable and consistent across a variety of specifications for the United States than for most countries. The perception of no adjustment existed for a time in the United States because too much was made of the decline in the exchange rate from its 1985 peak, while its equally large increase in the previous years was ignored. The exchange rate rise in early 1985 was never reflected in trade flows because it was too transitory in nature, given the long lags that exist in the adjustment of trade to changes in real exchange rates. Note, however, that changes in the U.S. trade balance, measured as a percentage of GDP, do require larger changes in real exchange rates than is the case for many European countries simply because the trade sector accounts for such a small share of the overall economy.

The empirical results also contradict the notion that Japanese trade is insensitive to market changes. On the contrary, Japan stands out with relatively large price and income elasticities, and it has clearly had the largest readjustment of its trade balance in recent years. Here, part of the problem may be that the critics have failed to take into account a concurrent decline in world oil prices that substantially cut Japan's oil import bill. If we focus only on that part of the Japanese current account that is strongly affected by the exchange rate—the nonenergy trade balance—the surplus built up rather steadily throughout the 1970s, and it dropped precipitously with the rise in the yen after 1985. That is, the trade adjustment is camouflaged in part by changes in the oil-trade balance in the opposite direction.

Finally, while variations in real exchange rates are found to have powerful effects on trade flows, these results do not suggest an integration of international markets in goods and services sufficient to support a fixed exchange rate regime. Without the ability to vary exchange rates, the realignment of the trade balance to shifts in saving-investment balances would be highly disruptive domestically, requiring large variations in relative rates of domestic inflation and employment.

TABLE 5A-1. *Regression Equations for Manufacturing Exports, Logarithms, 1970–90*

Country	Global imports	Relative price[a]	Time trend	R^2	Standard error	Durbin-Watson
United States	0.40	−1.12	1.61	0.976	0.048	1.1
	(1.7)	(5.8)	(1.3)			
Canada	0.49	0.21	2.89	0.993	0.035	1.1
	(5.4)	(1.0)	(4.5)			
Japan	1.45	−0.57	−1.63	0.998	0.054	1.1
	(5.5)	(3.1)	(1.0)			
Australia	0.46	−0.40	3.32	0.938	0.120	0.5
	(0.9)	(0.9)	(0.9)			
Large European countries						
France	1.30	−1.04	−2.74	0.993	0.023	1.7
	(8.3)	(3.2)	(3.3)			
Germany	1.06	−0.41	−1.22	0.994	0.026	1.3
	(5.4)	(1.6)	(1.1)			
United Kingdom	0.12	−0.71	3.75	0.959	0.048	0.8
	(0.5)	(5.2)	(2.6)			
Italy	0.51	−0.63	2.07	0.994	0.028	1.8
	(3.2)	(2.5)	(2.3)			
Small European countries						
Austria	0.85	−0.99	2.88	0.996	0.030	1.4
	(4.9)	(2.0)	(3.0)			
Belgium	1.40	−0.55	−6.47	0.992	0.019	1.6
	(6.7)	(4.6)	(6.7)			
Denmark	0.96	−1.06	0.09	0.996	0.023	1.6
	(5.1)	(7.4)	(0.8)			
Netherlands	1.39	−0.76	−2.20	0.989	0.039	1.2
	(5.8)	(2.9)	(1.7)			
Sweden	0.74	−1.04	−0.65	0.982	0.038	0.8
	(2.7)	(3.7)	(0.4)			

SOURCES: Author's calculations as explained in the text. T-statistics are in parentheses. Export and global imports are measured in constant prices.

a. Relative wholesale prices, except for France, where relative export prices are used.

TABLE 5A-2. *Constrained Regression Equations for Manufacturing Exports, Logarithms, 1970–90*

Country	Global imports	Relative price[a]	Time trend	Standard error	Durbin-Watson
United States	1.0	−0.74 (5.4)	−1.51 (7.5)	0.056	0.7
Canada	0.49 (5.4)	0.21 (1.0)	2.89 (4.5)	0.035	1.1
Japan	1.0	0.55 (2.8)	1.16 (4.7)	0.057	0.8
Australia	1.0	−0.44 (0.9)	−0.35 (0.9)	0.120	0.8
Large European countries					
France	1.0	−0.71 (2.4)	−1.18 (11.2)	0.025	0.9
Germany	1.0	−0.36 (2.1)	−0.87 (9.4)	0.025	1.4
United Kingdom	0.12 (0.5)	−0.71 (5.2)	3.75 (2.6)	0.048	0.8
Italy	0.51 (3.2)	−0.63 (2.5)	2.07 (2.3)	0.028	1.8
Small European countries					
Austria	1.0	−1.16 (2.5)	2.24 (3.9)	0.030	1.4
Belgium	1.0	−0.30 (2.7)	−3.55 (12.9)	0.023	1.1
Denmark	1.0	−1.11 (10.6)	[b]	0.023	1.5
Netherlands	1.0	−0.59 (3.8)	[b]	0.040	1.1
Sweden	1.0	−1.11 (4.1)	−2.14 (9.8)	0.038	0.7

SOURCES: Author's calculations as explained in the text. T-statistics are in parentheses. Exports and global imports are measured in constant prices.

a. Relative wholesale prices, except for France, where relative export prices are used.

b. Variables excluded from regression.

TABLE 5A-3. *Import of Manufactured Goods Using Industrial Production, 1970–90*

Country	Industrial production	Relative price	Time trend	R^2	Standard error	Durbin-Watson
United States	1.25	0.93	3.52	0.992	0.045	1.3
	(4.6)	(8.1)	(4.5)			
Canada[a]	1.46	0.86	1.63	0.995	0.024	2.0
	(11.61)	(7.5)	(5.9)			
Japan	1.86	1.25	1.21	0.991	0.061	1.1
	(5.9)	(5.8)	(1.0)			
Australia[a]	0.90	1.05	4.99	0.960	0.081	1.9
	(1.17)	(2.81)	(4.08)			
Large European countries						
France	1.51	0.82	3.81	0.997	0.025	1.7
	(10.7)	(5.3)	(15.7)			
Germany[a]	0.82	0.91	4.27	0.988	0.043	0.9
	(2.3)	(2.1)	(8.4)			
United Kingdom[a]	0.68	0.20	6.56	0.994	0.036	1.37
	(5.3)	(1.0)	(11.8)			
Italy[a]	1.38	1.42	3.65	0.993	0.034	1.6
	(7.4)	(6.9)	(8.5)			
Small European countries						
Austria	1.57	1.03	0.62	0.996	0.029	1.8
	(8.7)	(2.4)	(0.8)			
Belgium	1.03	0.55	4.08	0.992	0.027	2.5
	(5.9)	(4.0)	(7.8)			
Denmark[a]	1.49	0.07	− 1.35	0.984	0.028	2.0
	(7.7)	(0.4)	(2.3)			
Netherlands	1.75	0.32	0.32	0.991	0.027	1.7
	(7.0)	(1.1)	(0.7)			
Sweden[a]	1.09	1.04	2.65	0.991	0.029	2.1
	(6.2)	(4.5)	(11.2)			

SOURCES: Author's calculations as explained in the text. T-statistics are in parentheses. Imports and industrial production are measured in constant prices.
a. The relative price measure is constructed using the import price deflator.

References

Aldrich, Jonathan. 1982. "The Earnings Replacement Rate of Old-Age Benefits in 12 Countries, 1969–80." *Social Security Bulletin* 45 (November): 3–11.

Aliber, Robert Z. 1991. "U.S. Trade Deficit and the U.S. Fiscal Deficit: Cause and Effect." Department of Economics, University of Chicago.

Barro, Robert J. 1974. "Are Government Bonds Net Wealth?" *Journal of Political Economy* 82 (November–December): 1095–1117.

Bayoumi, Tamim, and Joseph Gagnon. 1992. "Taxation and Inflation: A New Explanation for Current Account Imbalances," International finance discussion paper 420. Washington: Board of Governors of the Federal Reserve System. January.

Bernheim, B. Douglas. 1987. "Ricardian Equivalence: An Evaluation of Theory and Evidence." In Stanley Fischer, ed., *NBER Macroeconomics Annual 1987.* MIT Press: 263–304.

Bilson, John F. O. 1978. "The Monetary Approach to the Exchange Rate: Some Empirical Evidence." *International Monetary Fund Staff Papers* 25 (March): 48–75.

Bosworth, Barry P., Gary Burtless, and John Sabelhaus. 1991. "The Decline in Saving: Evidence from Household Surveys." *Brookings Papers on Economic Activity 1:* 183–241.

Bosworth, Barry P., Andrew S. Carron, and Elisabeth H. Rhyne. 1987. *The Economics of Federal Credit Programs.* Brookings Institution.

Boughton, James M. 1988. *The Monetary Approach To Exchange Rates: What Now Remains?* Essays in international finance 171. Princeton University, Department of Economics, October.

Bryant, Ralph C., and others, eds. 1988. *Empirical Macroeconomics for Interdependent Economies.* Brookings Institution.

Campbell, John Y., and Richard H. Clarida. 1987. "The Dollar and Real Interest Rates." *Carnegie-Rochester Conference Series on Public Policy* 27 (Autumn): 103–39.

Carroll, Christopher D., and Lawrence H. Summers. 1991. "Consumption Growth Parallels Income Growth: Some New Evidence." In B. Douglas Bernheim and John Shoven, eds., *National Saving and Economic Performance,* University of Chicago Press.

Corden, W. M. 1986. *Inflation, Exchange Rates and the World Economy: Lectures on International Monetary Economics,* 3d ed. University of Chicago Press.

David, Paul A., and John L Scadding. 1974. "Private Savings: Ultrarationality, Aggregation, and 'Denison's Law.'" *Journal of Political Economy* 82 (March–April): 225–49.

Dean, Andrew, and others. 1990. "Saving Trends and Behaviour in OECD Countries." *OECD Economic Studies,* no. 14 (Spring): 7–58.

Dornbusch, Rudiger. 1980a. "Exchange Rate Economics: Where Do We Stand?" *Brookings Papers on Economic Activity 1*: 143–85.

———. 1980b. *Open Economy Macroeconomics.* Basic Books.

———. 1976. "Expectations and Exchange Rate Dynamics." *Journal of Political Economy* 84 (December): 1161–76.

Egebo, Thomas, Pete Richardson, and Ian Lienert. 1990. "A Model of Housing Investment for the Major OECD Economies." *OECD Economic Studies,* no. 14 (Spring): 151–88.

Farrell, M. J. 1970. "The Magnitude of 'Rate-of-Growth' Effects on Aggregate Savings." *Economic Journal* 80 (December): 873–94.

Feldstein, Martin S. 1980. "International Differences in Social Security and Saving." *Journal of Public Economics* 14 (October): 225–44.

———. 1983. "Domestic Saving and International Capital Movements in the Long Run and the Short Run." *European Economic Review* 21 (March–April): 129–51.

———. 1987. "Correcting the Trade Deficit." *Foreign Affairs* 65 (Spring): 795–806.

Feldstein, Martin S., and Charles Horioka. 1980. "Domestic Saving and International Capital Flows." *Economic Journal* 90 (June): 314–29.

Fisher, P. G., and others. 1990. "Econometric Evaluation of the Exchange Rate in Models of the UK Economy." *Economic Journal* 100 (December): 1230–44.

Flavin, Marjorie A. 1981. "The Adjustment of Consumption to Changing Expectations about Future Income." *Journal of Political Economy* 89 (October): 974–1009.

Fleming, J. Marcus. 1962. "Domestic Financial Policies under Fixed and under Floating Exchange Rates." *International Monetary Fund Staff Papers* 9 (November): 369–79.

Ford, Robert, and Pierre Poret. 1991. "Business Investment: Recent Performance and Some Implications for Policy." *OECD Economic Studies,* no. 16 (Spring): 79–131. An expanded version of this study is available as OECD working paper 88 (November 1990).

Frankel, Jeffrey A. 1983. "Monetary and Portfolio-Balance Models of Exchange Rate Determination." In Jagdeep S. Bhandari and Bluford H. Putnam, eds., *Economic Interdependence and Flexible Exchange Rates.* MIT Press: 84–115.

————. 1986. "International Capital Mobility and Crowding-out in the United States Economy: Imperfect Integration of Financial Markets or Goods Markets." In R. W. Hafer, ed., *How Open Is the U.S. Economy?* Lexington, Mass.: Lexington Books: 33–68.

————. 1990. "International Financial Integration, Relations among Interest Rates and Exchange Rates, and Monetary Indicators." In Charles A. Pigott, ed., *International Financial Integration and U.S. Monetary Policy.* Federal Reserve Bank of New York: 15–58.

Frenkel, Jacob A. 1976. "A Monetary Approach to the Exchange Rate: Doctrinal Aspects and Empirical Evidence." *Scandinavian Journal of Economics* 78 (2): 200-24.

Frenkel, Jacob A., and Michael L. Mussa. 1985. "Asset Markets, Exchange Rates, and the Balance of Payments." In Ronald W. Jones and Peter B. Kenen, eds., *Handbook of International Economics,* vol 2. North-Holland: 679–747.

Frenkel, Jacob A., and Assaf Razin. 1987. "The Mundell-Fleming Model a Quarter Century Later: A Unified Exposition." *International Monetary Fund Staff Papers* 34 (December): 567–620.

Friedman, Benjamin M. 1978. "Crowding Out or Crowding In? Economic Consequences of Financing Government Deficits." *Brookings Papers on Economic Activity 3,* 593–641.

Gagnon, Joseph E., and Andrew K. Rose. 1990. "Why Hasn't Trade Grown Faster than Income? Inter-industry Trade over the Past Century." International finance discussion paper 371. Washington: Board of Governors of the Federal Reserve System. January.

Goldstein, Morris, and Mohsin S. Khan. 1985. "Income and Price Effects in Foreign Trade." In Ronald W. Jones and Peter B. Kenen, eds., *Handbook of International Economics,* vol 2. North-Holland.

Gylfason, Thorvaldur, and John F. Helliwell. 1983. "A Synthesis of Keynesian, Monetary, and Portfolio Approaches to Flexible Exchange Rates." *Economic Journal* 93 (December): 820–31.

Hayashi, Fumio. 1982. "The Permanent Income Hypothesis: Estimation and Testing by Instrumental Variables." *Journal of Political Economy* 90 (October): 895–916.

————. 1986. "Why Is Japan's Saving Rate So Apparently High?" In Stanley Fischer, ed., *NBER Macroeconomics Annual 1986.* MIT Press: 147–210.

Hayashi, Fumio, Albert Ando, and Richard Ferris. 1988. "Life Cycle and Bequest Savings: A Study of Japanese and U.S. Households Based on Data from the 1984 NSFIE and the 1983 Survey of Consumer Finances." *Journal of the Japanese and International Economy* 2 (December): 450–91.

Heller, Peter S. 1989. "Aging, Savings, and Pensions in the Group of Seven Countries: 1980–2025." *Journal of Public Policy* 9 (April–June): 127–55.

Hill, Peter. 1984. "Inflation, Holding Gains and Saving." *OECD Economic Studies,* no. 2 (Spring): 151–64.

Hooper, Peter. 1988. "Exchange Rates and U.S. External Adjustment in the Short Run and the Long Run." Brookings discussion paper in International Economics 65. October.

Hooper, Peter, and Catherine Mann. 1989. "Exchange Rate Pass-through in the 1980s: The Case of U.S. Imports of Manufactures." *Brookings Papers on Economic Activity 1:* 297–329.

Hooper, Peter, and John Morton. 1982. "Fluctuations in the Dollar: A Model of Nominal and Real Exchange Rate Determination." *Journal of International Money and Finance* 1 (April): 39–56.

Horioka, Charles Y. 1989a. "Why is Japan's Private Saving Rate So High?" In Ryuzo Sato and Takashi Negishi, eds., *Developments in Japanese Economics.* San Diego: Academic Press, 145–78.

———. 1989b. "The Determinants of Japan's Saving Rate." Institute of Social and Economic Research, Osaka University, discussion paper 189. June.

Houthakker, Hendrik S., and Stephen P. Magee. 1969. "Income and Price Elasticities in World Trade." *Review of Economics and Statistics* 51 (May): 111–25.

Inter-American Development Bank. 1992. *Economic and Social Progress in Latin America, 1992 Report.* Washington.

International Monetary Fund. 1987. *Report on the World Current Account Discrepancy.* Washington. September.

Isard, Peter. 1988. "Exchange Rate Modeling: An Assessment of Alternative Approaches." In Ralph C. Bryant and others, eds., *Empirical Macroeconomics for Interdependent Economies.* Brookings Institution.

Ishikawa, Tsuneo. 1988. "Saving and Labor Supply of Aged Households in Japan." *Journal of the Japanese and International Economy* 2 (December): 417–49.

Johnson, Harry G. 1958. *International Trade and Economic Growth.* London: George Allen and Unwin.

Krugman, Paul R. 1989a. *Exchange-Rate Instability.* MIT Press.

———.1989b. "Differences in Income Elasticities and Trends in Real Exchange Rates." *European Economic Review* 33 (May): 1031-46.

Krugman, Paul R., and Richard E. Baldwin. 1987. "The Persistence of the U.S. Trade Deficit." *Brookings Papers on Economic Activity 1:* 1–43.

Kuttner, Robert. 1991. *The End of Laissez-Faire: National Economics Purpose and the Global Economy after the Cold War.* Knopf.

Lawrence, Robert Z. 1979. "Toward a Better Understanding of Trade Balance Trends: The Cost-Price Puzzle." *Brookings Papers on Economic Activity, 1:1979,* 191–212.

———. 1990. "U.S. Current Account Adjustment: An Appraisal." *Brookings Papers on Economic Activity 2:* 343–82.

McKibbin, Warwick J., and Jeffrey D. Sachs. 1991. *Global Linkages: Macroeconomic Interdependence and Cooperation in the World Economy.* Brookings Institution.

McKinnon, Ronald I. 1984. *An International Standard for Monetary Stabilization.* Washington: Institute for International Economics.

Marris, Stephen. 1985. *Deficits and the Dollar: The World Economy at Risk.* Washington: Institute for International Economics.

Marston, Richard C. 1985. "Stabilization Policies in Open Economies." In Ronald W. Jones and Peter B. Kenen, eds., *Handbook of International Economics,* vol 2. North-Holland.

———. 1986. "Real Exchange Rates and Productivity Growth in the United States and Japan." National Bureau of Economic Research working paper 1922.

———. 1990. "Pricing to Market in Japanese Manufacturing." *Journal of International Economics* 29 (November): 217–36.

Meese, Richard A.. and Kenneth Rogoff. 1983. "Empirical Exchange Rate Models of the Seventies: Do They Fit out of Sample?" *Journal of International Economics* 14 (February): 3–24.

———. 1988. "Was It Real? The Exchange Rate-Interest Differential Relation over the Modern Floating-Rate Period." *Journal of Finance* 43 (September): 933–48.

Modigliani, Franco. 1966. "The Life Cycle Hypothesis of Saving, the Demand for Wealth and the Supply of Capital." *Social Research* 33 (Summer): 160–217.

———. 1970. "The Life Cycle Hypothesis of Saving and Intercountry Differences in the Saving Ratio." In W. A. Eltis, M. FG. Scott, and J. N. Wolfe, eds., *Induction, Growth and Trade: Essays in Honour of Sir Roy Harrod.* Oxford, England: Clarendon Press: 197–225.

———. 1986. "Life Cycle, Individual Thrift, and the Wealth of Nations," *American Economic Review* 76 (June): 297–313.

Modigliani, Franco, and Arlie Sterling. 1983. "Determinants of Private Saving with Special Reference to the Role of Social Security—Cross-Country Tests." In Franco Modigliani and Richard Hemming, eds., *The Determinants of National Saving and Wealth.* St. Martin's Press.

Morgan Guaranty Trust Company. 1983. "Effective Exchange Rates: Update and Refinement." *World Financial Markets* (August): 6–13.

———. 1986. "Dollar Index Confusion." *World Financial Markets* (October–November): 14–19.

Muller, Patrice, and Robert W. R. Price. 1984. "Structural Budget Deficits and Fiscal Stance." OECD working paper 15. Paris. July.

Mundell, Robert. A. 1963. "Capital Mobility and Stabilization Policy under Fixed and Flexible Exchange Rates." *Canadian Journal of Economics and Political Science* 29: 475–85.

———. 1991. "The Great Exchange Rate Controversy: Trade Balances and the International Monetary System." In C. Fred Bergsten, ed., *International Adjustment and Financing.* Washington: Institute for International Economics: 187–238.

Mussa, Michael L. 1976. "The Exchange Rate, the Balance of Payments and Monetary and Fiscal Policy under a Regime of Controlled Floating." *Scandinavian Journal of Economics* 78:2 229–48.

Organization for Economic Cooperation and Development. 1987a. "Total Factor Productivity." *OECD Economic Outlook* 42 (December): 39–49.

———. 1987b. *Purchasing Power Parities and Real Expenditures, 1985.*

———. 1991a. *Labor Force Statistics, 1969–89.* Paris.

———. 1991b. *National Accounts,* vol 2. Data tape. Paris.

———. 1991c. *OECD Economic Outlook, Statistics on Microcomputer Diskette.* Paris. July.

Roubini, Nouriel, and Jeffrey Sachs. 1989. "Government Spending and Budget Deficits in the Industrial Countries." *Economic Policy: A European Forum* 8 (April): 99–132.

Scholl, Russell B. 1991. "The International Investment Position of the United States in 1990." *Survey of Current Business* 71 (June): 23–35.

Summers, Lawrence H. 1981. "Capital Taxation and Accumulation in a Life Cycle Growth Model." *American Economic Review* 71 (September): 533–44.

Tesar, Linda L. 1991. "Saving, Investment and International Capital Flows." *Journal of International Economics* 31 (August): 55–78.

Tobin, James. 1967. "Life Cycle Saving and Balanced Growth." In *Ten Economic Studies in the Tradition of Irving Fisher.* John Wiley: 231–56.

———. 1983. "Comment on Domestic Saving and International Capital Movements in the Long Run and the Short Run." *European Economic Review* 21 (March–April): 153–56.

Tobin, James, and Jorge Braga De Macedo. 1980. "The Short-run Macroeconomics of Floating Exchange Rates: An Exposition." In John S. Chipman and Charles P. Kindleberger., eds., *Flexible Exchange Rates and the Balance of Payments.* North-Holland: 5–28.

Ueda, Kasuo. 1987. "Investment Savings Balance and the Japanese Current Account Surplus." Japan Center for International Finance, policy study series, no. 7. May.

Westphal, Uwe. 1983. "Comment: Domestic Saving and International Capital Movements in the Long Run and the Short Run by M. Feldstein." *European Economic Review* 21 (March–April): 157–59.

Index